HODDER SCIENCE

Pupil's Book

Nigel Heslop George Snape
James Williams Marguerite Hall
David Brodie

Hodder & Stoughton
A MEMBER OF THE HODDER HEADLINE GROUP

Photo acknowledgements

The publishers would like to thank the following individuals, institutions and companies for permission to reproduce photographs in this book. Every effort has been made to trace ownership of copyright. The publishers would be happy to make arrangements with any copyright holder whom it has not been possible to contact:

Action Plus (23 bottom, 69, 71 left, 76, 108); All Action (83); Andrew Lambert (21 bottom, 63, 70 left, 98, 103, 107 all, 109); Associated Press (139); BBC Natural History Unit (78, 126 top right); Bruce Coleman Limited (32 middle right, 43 all, 71 right, 79, 91, 122, 126 left and middle and bottom right, 127 middle and bottom left, 127 both bottom right); Corbis (7, 20 left; 32 bottom right, 88, 110, 128, 138 bottom); David & Helen Litt (85 left); Galaxy Picture Library (147 bottom right); Hodder & Stoughton (33 bottom, 145); Holt Studios (29, 85 both right, 89 both, 127 top left); Home Office (138 top); Hulton Getty (23 top); Life File (22 both right, 32 bottom left, 55 top right, 66 left, 67, 95, 97, 112, 113, 129 middle and bottom, 134 top, 135, 136 left, 142); Natural History Museum (33 top); Nigel Heslop (20 top right, 25, 102, 134 bottom, 136 right); Oxford Scientific Films (5 all, 123); Photodisc (141); Press Association (58); Ronald Grant (130); Science Museum, Science & Society Picture Library (2); Science Photo Library (20 bottom right, 21 top, 32 top and middle left and top right, 33 middle, 47, 48 all, 55 both left and bottom right, 62, 70 right, 106, 114, 118 all, 119 both, 121 all, 127 top right, 129 top, 143, 144 both, 146 all, 147 all left and top and middle right); Sue Cunningham (66 right); Wellcome Trust (8, 22 left)

Orders: please contact Bookpoint Ltd, 130 Milton Park, Abingdon, Oxon OX14 4SB. Telephone: (44) 01235 827720. Fax: (44) 01235 400454. Lines are open from 9.00–6.00, Monday to Saturday, with a 24 hour message answering service.

You can also order through our website www.hodderheadline.co.uk

British Library Cataloguing in Publication Data
A catalogue record for this title is available from the British Library

ISBN 0 340 80438 6

First published 2002
Impression number   10 9 8 7 6 5 4
Year   2008 2007 2006 2005 2004 2003

Copyright © 2002 Nigel Heslop, James Williams, David Brodie, George Snape, Marguerite Hall

Cover photo from Holt Studios International.
Typeset by Fakenham Photosetting.
Printed in Italy for Hodder & Stoughton Educational, a division of Hodder Headline, 338 Euston Road, London NW1 3BH.

Contents

Preface

Hodder Science is a collection of resources designed to match exactly the QCA exemplar Scheme of Work for KS3. The core material of the series is suitable for the more able two-thirds of pupils. The scheme has successfully moved away from the minimalist approach of the past decade, is pupil-friendly and easy to read.

Hodder Science Gold has been written to extend the range of the *Hodder Science* series, specifically catering for the lower 30–35% of the ability range. These books will progressively target levels 2 to 4/5 of the National Curriculum.

Hodder Science Gold takes a new attitude to producing books for the lower attainer. It does far more than just present the same learning material at a slightly lower reading age. Marguerite Hall, a well-known learning methods consultant, has lent her expertise to increase the friendliness of the text and the accessibility of the way the ideas are presented. We have taken an integrated approach to producing material aimed at low attainers for the 21st Century.

- Key words boxes highlight and define target vocabulary on the spread where the terms are first used.
- Concepts are introduced at a level and rate more suitable for slower learners.
- Progression, through the concepts and models used, is tailored to the needs of a slower learner.
- There is no compromise on essential learning vocabulary, but peripheral vocabulary is kept to a simple reading level.
- Reading level concentrates on good sentence structure to make the flow of reading easier.
- Sometimes a few more simple words are used to explain a difficult concept rather than rigidly cutting word count.
- Generally word count per page is one half to two thirds of the parallel *Hodder Science* books.
- The number and style of questions has been altered to enable slower pupils to keep pace.
- Essential summary tasks contain a high level of prompt to ensure accuracy and success.
- To aid parallel use of the books, the spread by spread structure exactly mirrors the higher level books.
- To avoid stigmatisation of the lower attainer, many illustrations are the same and the book colour is the same. The gold trim signifies that these books are special.

Nigel Heslop 2002

CHAPTER 1

Life

What are living things made from?

All living things are made up of **cells**. A group of cells makes up a **tissue**. A group of tissues makes up an **organ**. A group of organs makes up an **organ system**. Your body is made up of millions of cells.

Heart
This organ pumps blood around the body.

Liver
This organ cleans the blood.

Kidney
These organs take liquid waste (urine) out of our blood.

Small intestine
This organ finishes digesting our food.

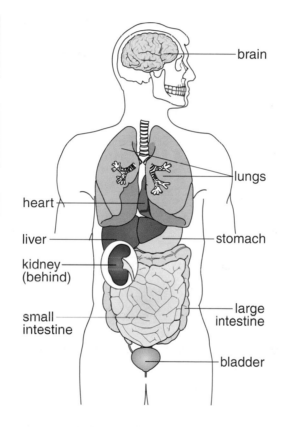

Brain
This organ controls the whole body.

Lungs
These organs are used for breathing.

Stomach
This organ starts to digest our food.

Large intestine
This organ carries our solid waste out and puts water back into the blood.

Bladder
This organ stores urine.

Questions

1 Which organ controls the whole body?

2 Which two organs digest the food we eat?

3 Which organ cleans the blood?

4 What do we call a group of cells?

5 What are organs made up of?

6 Copy or trace the outline of the body into your book. Close the textbook, then try to remember where the organs are and label them. Check your answers with the textbook.

Cells

Key words

cell   The smallest unit of any living thing or organism

cell membrane   Lets substances into and out of the cell

cytoplasm   A jelly-like substance where chemical reactions take place in the cell

nucleus   Controls what the cell does

Robert Hooke

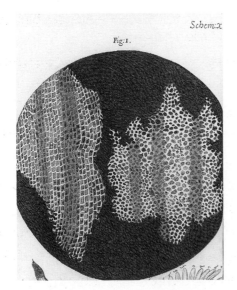

Figure 1 Hooke's drawing of the cells in cork

Robert Hooke

In 1665 a scientist called Robert Hooke looked at pieces of cork under a microscope. He could see tiny box shapes. He thought that they looked like the little rooms that monks lived in, called **cells**. But cells are not like boxes. They are not solid or empty. They are more like plastic bags full of jelly. We can build a model of a cell using jelly. Look at Hooke's drawing in Figure 1. It looks like a brick wall. Each brick is a cell.

Robert Hooke used a simple microscope. The word microscope means an instrument for looking at small things. When you see the term micro it means 'very small'. The term scope means an 'instrument for observing'.

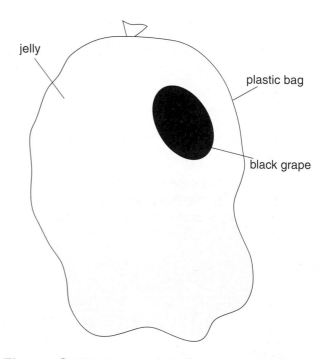

Figure 2 This is a model of an animal cell made from jelly.

Cell structure

Plants and animals have cells. Plant cells are similar to animal cells, but there are some differences between the cells. Look at the cells in Figure 3. Work out what things are the same and what things are different.

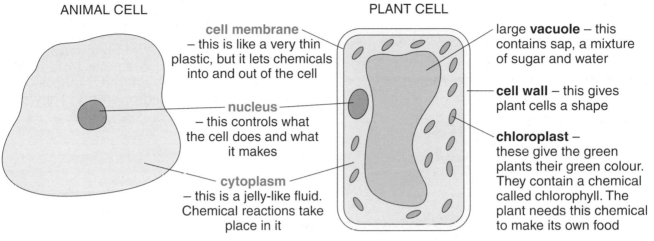

ANIMAL CELL

PLANT CELL

cell membrane – this is like a very thin plastic, but it lets chemicals into and out of the cell

large **vacuole** – this contains sap, a mixture of sugar and water

nucleus – this controls what the cell does and what it makes

cell wall – this gives plant cells a shape

cytoplasm – this is a jelly-like fluid. Chemical reactions take place in it

chloroplast – these give the green plants their green colour. They contain a chemical called chlorophyll. The plant needs this chemical to make its own food

Figure 3 An animal cell and a plant cell.

Questions

1 Why are cells not like boxes?

2 Which part of a cell is like the plastic bag in the model?

3 Which part of a cell is like the jelly in the model?

4 Which part of a cell is like the black grape in the model?

5 Copy the table below into your exercise book under the heading 'Cells'. Put a tick if the part is present in the cell and a cross if it is not. Use the diagrams to help you.

Cell structure	Animal cell	Plant cell
cell membrane	✓	✓
cell wall		
cytoplasm		
nucleus		
large vacuole		
chloroplast		

6 Plants have a cell wall that helps to give the cell a shape. What do humans have to give them support and shape?

7 Which part of a plant or animal cell controls what it does?

Remember

Copy and complete the sentences below. Use these words:

cells   cell wall   large vacuole   nucleus   cytoplasm

All living things are made up of **c____**. Humans may contain over a million, million cells. Plant and animal cells have a cell membrane, a **n_____** and cytoplasm. Plant cells also have a **c____ w___, c_____**, and a **l____ v_____**. Cells are controlled by the nucleus. Chemical reactions, which keep the cell alive, take place in the **c_____**.

Tissues

Key words

sterile Very clean conditions
tissue A group of similar cells
tissue culture Growing tissues outside the body

Different cells, different jobs!

Different cells have different jobs. Some cells make things. Some cells control things. Some cells protect us. Some cells give us support. They often work together in groups called **tissues**.

Animal tissues	Job
skin (this is also an organ)	to protect the body and stop harmful things entering
blood	to carry oxygen, carbon dioxide and chemicals from food around the body
bone	to give support
nerves	to carry messages
muscle	to help us move

Plant tissues	Job
xylem	to carry water and minerals from the roots to the leaves
phloem	to carry food dissolved in water around the plant

Table 1 Some animal and plant tissues.

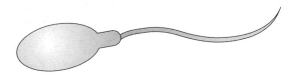

a) a sperm cell

c) a red blood cell from above and cut in half to show the shape

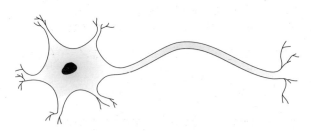

b) a nerve cell

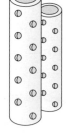

d) xylem vessels

Figure 1 Plant and animal cells come in different shapes and sizes.

Growing tissues

Some animals and plants can replace damaged parts and tissues. Humans do this when we repair cuts and broken bones. If we have a deep cut that we cannot repair properly we make scar tissue. Large parts of plants can be cut off without the plant dying. Gardeners call it pruning.

If a large fish eats one arm of a starfish, the starfish can grow another arm. The photographs in Figure 2 show this happening. Humans cannot grow missing arms or even fingers. Some people think that cutting a worm in two will give you two worms. This is not true. The top half may grow a new tail part, but the tail end will die.

We can grow some tissues in the laboratory. When tissues are grown like this they are called **tissue cultures**. They have to be grown in very clean or **sterile** conditions.

Figure 2 This starfish is growing another arm

New cells from old

Growth

The cells in your body are being replaced all the time. Normal cells do not live forever and in time they will die. New ones will take their place. Since you were born you have grown. In fact you no longer have any of the cells in your body that you were born with! As we grow, the cells, tissues and organs in our body also grow and change. The cells in our body divide to make new cells. This is called **cell division**.

The nucleus in the cell controls what the cell does (its **function**) and when and how it should divide.

Questions

1   Which part of a cell controls how and when it divides?

Look at the cartoon strip to see how cells divide. Cells make copies of themselves when they divide.

a) The cell prepares to divide.

b) The nucleus makes a copy of itself.

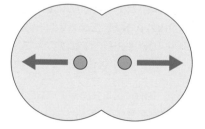

c) The two nuclei (the word for more than one nucleus) move to opposite ends of the cell and the cell starts to pinch in the middle.

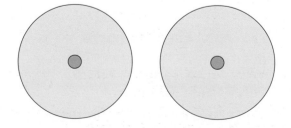

d) Two new cells are produced identical to the first cell.

Figure 1

Can all cells divide?

Not all cells can divide or repair themselves. Red blood cells are made in bone marrow. When red blood cells are made they lose their nucleus before going into our bloodstream. As they travel around the body they cannot divide. If they did divide they could block our blood vessels. Nerve cells are another type of cell that cannot divide. If nerve cells are damaged, they cannot repair themselves.

Figure 2 The actor Christopher Reeve was paralysed in a horse riding accident. He damaged his nervous system in the accident and hasn't been able to walk since. This is because nerve cells can't repair themselves when damaged.

Questions

2   Red blood cells do not divide as they travel around our blood vessels. Why can't they divide?

3   What could happen if red blood cells divided as they travelled in our bloodstream?

4   Imagine that you badly cut your hand and cut through nerve cells leading to the fingers. What might happen?

Remember

In the paragraph below, decide which word from each pair of words is the correct one. Copy the correct paragraph into your exercise book.

Cells do not live **long/forever**. As we grow, our cells **divide/add** to make new cells. The cell is controlled by the **nucleus/cytoplasm**. Some cells cannot **add/divide**. **Muscle/Nerve** cells are an example of these sorts of cells. When cells divide an exact copy is made.

Cancer

What is cancer?

When cells can't stop dividing we call it **cancer**. The cells form a lump called a **tumour**. Cancerous cells can also travel around the body in the bloodstream. This can cause new tumours to grow at other places in the body.

Many things can cause cancer, for example too much sunbathing or being exposed to radioactivity or strong chemicals.

Questions

1   In your own words explain what cancer is.

2   What is a tumour?

How do we treat cancer?

Not all cancers will kill you. Many cancers can be treated if we find them early enough. We have three ways of treating cancer. The first two are what we call a therapy. The word therapy means treatment. Although being exposed to radioactivity can cause cancer, we can also use it to kill cancer cells. The radioactivity is targeted at the cancer cells, leaving healthy cells alone.

1   *Radiotherapy* (killing the cancer cells by treating them with radioactivity)

2   *Chemotherapy* (killing the cancer cells by treating them with powerful chemicals)

3   *Surgery* (cutting the cancer cells out of the body).

You are very unlikely to have cancer as a child or young person. The older you are, the greater the chance of having some type of cancer. Cancer is not just found in humans. Cats, dogs, farm animals, birds and fish can all suffer from cancer.

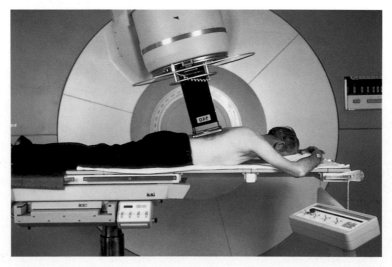

Figure 1 A person having radiotherapy.

There are lots of different types of cancer. The graph shows how common they are.

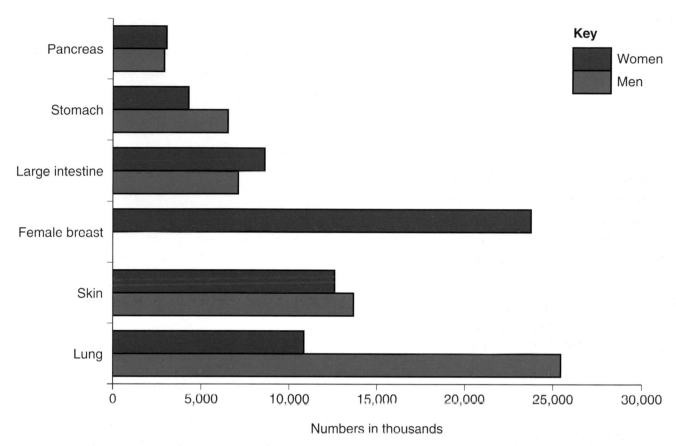

Figure 2 This graph shows how common different kinds of cancer are in men and women.

Questions

3 What do you think it means when a person is called a therapist? Try to complete the following sentences:

A physiotherapist is a person who

_____

A speech therapist is a person who

_____

4 There are more cases of skin cancer today than there were 50 years ago. Why do you think this is? (*Hint*: Think about holidays!)

Remember

Chose the right meaning for the words below from this list:

tumour   therapy   cancer

a) This means treatment.

b) This means that cells are dividing uncontrollably.

c) This means a lump or collection of cancerous cells.

Are you irreplaceable?

1.5

Key words

organ   A group of tissues working together to do a particular job

transplant   Replacing a damaged organ or organs with healthy ones

Organ transplants

We cannot re-grow limbs or **organs**, unlike the starfish on page 5. If our organs become damaged, we may need an organ **transplant**. The kidneys, heart, liver, lungs, corneas (the clear part at the front of the eye), heart valves and bones can all be transplanted. Skin can also be used to treat patients with severe burns.

Body part	How can you live without it?
A Skull cap	Metal plates can be used to protect the brain.
B Arms and legs	You can have a replacement false limb fitted.
C Liver	You can live without most of your liver. In children the liver can sometimes grow back!
D Appendix	Lots of people have their appendix out with no problems as a result.
E Gall bladder	This produces bile that neutralises acid added to the food in your stomach. You have to be careful what you eat, but you can live without it.
F Pancreas	This makes substances that break down food. If this is removed, you have to take medication for the rest of your life.
G Stomach	Most of your stomach can go.
H Large intestine	A lot of the large intestine can be taken away.
I Small intestine	Most of the digestion of your food happens here. The small intestine is several feet long and you could lose most of it.
J Kidney	You have two kidneys. One will do the work of making urine.
K Reproductive organs	None of these are needed and can be removed. They produce chemicals called hormones so you will need to take medication.

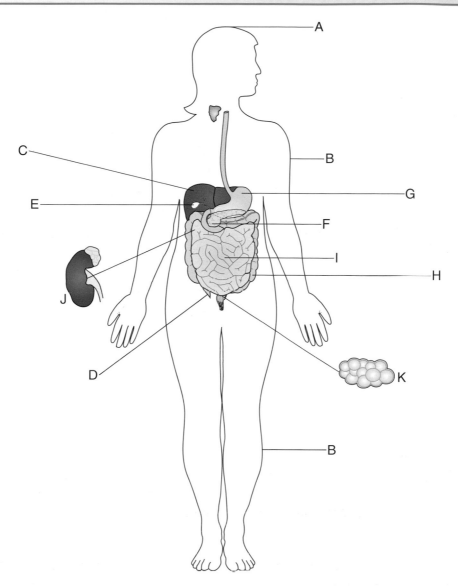

Figure 1 These are the bits of your body that you can live without

Questions

1 Which two parts of the body in the list, if removed, would mean that you have to take medicines?

2 Which pair of organs in the list can we lose one of and still live normally?

3 Name two essential organs of the body (not in the list) that you CANNOT live without.

Remember

Choose the correct word from each pair of words to complete the paragraph. Copy the correct paragraph into your exercise book.

When an organ is damaged, it may be possible to carry out a **removal/transplant**. The organs that can be **donated/taken** include the heart, lungs, kidneys, pancreas and liver. Tissues that can be donated include corneas, skin, bone, heart valves and connective tissues.

Finishing off!

Remember

Plants and animals are made up of **cells**. There are many different types of cell. Cells have a **nucleus** that controls what the cell does. The nucleus also controls when and how cells divide to form new ones.

Groups of cells make up **tissues**. Groups of tissues make up **organs**. Groups of organs make up **organ systems**. These are the organ systems found in humans:

As we grow, our cells divide making exact copies of themselves. As the number of cells increases and their size increases, we grow larger.

When cells cannot stop dividing, we call it **cancer**. Many cancers can be treated.

We can live without some parts of our bodies. Some parts can be transplanted from a donor.

Life processes	Organ system
Movement	Muscles and skeleton
Respiration	Lungs and cells
Sensitivity	Nervous system
Growth	Digestive system
Reproduction	Reproductive system
Excretion	Digestive, urinary and respiratory
Nutrition	Digestive system

Questions

1 Take a new page in your exercise book. Make a list of all the Key Words from the boxes in this chapter down the side. Take two lines per word. Try to write the meaning of each word without looking. Then go back and fill in any you did not know or got wrong.

2 What function (job) do the following organs have:
   a) brain   c) liver
   b) skin   d) kidneys?

3 What function do the following tissues have:
   a) phloem   c) nerves
   b) bone   d) xylem?

4 Which tissue in humans and animals is also an organ?

Web sites to visit:

Cells alive
   http://www.cellsalive.com/

The Why Files – stem cells
   http://whyfiles.org/shorties/stem_cell.html

Changes

CHAPTER 2

Starter Activity
On the state line

In Mandy's roadside cafe they use lots of materials. The materials are all different, they do different things. The things they do are called **properties**. The properties of the materials make each one useful. Each one is useful in a different way. Some of the materials are **mixtures**, but others are **pure** substances.

Solids, **liquids** and **gases** are the three basic **states of matter**. Matter is another word for all the 'stuff' we know makes up our world. Solids, liquids and gases can change state.

- **Melting** is turning from a solid to a liquid.
- **Boiling** (or evaporating) is turning from a liquid to a gas.

Questions

1 Copy this table and fill it in for all the materials labelled in the picture.

Solid	Liquid	Gas

2 Explain how you know if a material is a solid, liquid or gas.

3 In the picture, the wax of the candle on the table is melting. How can you tell by looking if a material is melting?

4 The water inside the coffee maker is boiling. How can you tell by looking if a material is boiling?

Carnival people

Key words

gas A material that escapes everywhere

liquid A wet, runny material that takes the shape of a container

material The stuff everything is made from

solid A material that keeps its shape

A wild time

Figure 1 Carnival at the Sambadrome. All matter is made of tiny particles. The particles move about constantly, even in solids.

The particles in a **material** are tiny. They are smaller than anything you could imagine – far too small to see. But all particles are moving all the time.

They behave rather like the people at a crowded carnival.

Solid in the stand

The particles in a **solid** are like the people in the stands at a carnival. Each person has a fixed place and the people next to them do not change position. The people have no spaces between them. They are all in neat blocks. The people can move about a little, backwards and forwards, to and fro, but they do not move out of their fixed position. The block of people always stays the same shape, even though they are moving.

1   Imagine you are in the stands at the carnival. Explain how you could move about a little without leaving your seat.

Liquid crowds

The people standing in the crowd at the carnival are like the jumble of particles in a **liquid**. They are all pushed together so that there are no spaces between them. The people can move past each other. The people can move quite a lot. They can have different people next to them. They can move past each other to get to a different place. Just like particles in a liquid they will fill up whatever space they are put in. It could be a long, thin pavement or a square space. They will take the shape of the 'container'. Here it is the fence that holds the crowd in its shape.

Questions

2   Draw a picture of the people standing in the crowd as a random jumble of people all pushed together.

Performers are a gas

Gas particles are like the people dancing. They are all moving about very quickly and often bump into each other.

Gases need to be kept in a container. This is because the particles move about so much. The container is like the fence at the sides of the procession. Gases mix easily with each other. That is how a smell spreads through air.

Questions

3   A gas would be like people running round the school hall. Draw a picture of this.

Remember

Copy these sentences and draw particle pictures to show what they mean.

- Particles in a **solid** are touching each other. They have fixed positions but move a little.
- Particles in a **liquid** are pushed together and touching as well. They move about at random.
- Particles in a **gas** are separate from each other. They move about very quickly.

A closer look at carnival people

Key words

compress You can squash something into a smaller space

energy This makes things happen

If you make the people more excited – like when there is louder music – then the people move about more. This is like making a solid more 'excited' by giving it energy. This makes its temperature higher and its particles move faster.

Packed solid

Figure 1 Watching the carnival from the stands

On the previous page you thought of particles of matter as people in a carnival. This is to help you make a picture happen in your head. All the particles in solids, liquids and gases have some **energy** stored in them. The energy is stored as movement. The particles are moving all the time, even in solids.

This idea can be used to explain things – like what is happening when a solid heats up.

Liquid crowds

Figure 2 Standing in the crowd at the carnival

Imagine the people pushing past each other to see the procession. They move like the particles in a liquid. Look at the pictures, then shut your eyes and make the people move in your head.

The dancers

There are big gaps between the performers. So two parts of the carnival can mix together if they need to. Or the carnival procession could go through a narrower space if it needs to. This is like squashing a gas. Gases are easy to **compress**.

Figure 3 Dancers at the carnival

Questions

Copy and complete the sentences using the word list.

> **solid   particle   compressed
> closer   shape**

1   Solids don't mix because each **p**_____ has its own place.

2   Liquids stay the same volume because the particles can't be pushed **c**_____ together.

3   Liquids don't keep their **s**_____ when put into another jug.

4   Pieces of **s**_____ stay the same shape even if they are put in a different dish.

5   A gas can be **c**_____ because its particles can be pushed closer.

Remember

Copy this paragraph into your book.

You can think how people behave at a Carnival. They move more as they get more excited. The movement of the people is like the energy that makes material hot.

Hard, heavy lessons

Figure 1 This is what would happen if you tried to saw metal with a wooden saw

Hardness

Some materials are easy to cut and some are hard. **Hardness** means how strongly the particles in a solid hold on to each other. Wood and plastic are easier to cut than metal. The force that holds the particles together is strong in metals and weak in wood and plastic.

Soft materials like wax, plasticene and clay have particles that hold on to each other very weakly. So they can be squashed into a new shape. But if you bake clay models in a kiln, you get a change which makes a very strong force between the particles. Baked clay is very hard.

1 Why do we use a saw made of metal to cut wood?

2 What do you think the order of hardness is for these materials. Start with the hardest:

> **dry clay**   **steel drill**   **brick**
> **candle wax**   **stone**   **soap**

Density

Metal objects like tools are often heavier for their size than other objects. This is because the metal particles are heavy and are packed very closely together.

The property 'heaviness for its size' has a name. Its called **density**. We measure it in grams per cubic centimetre. This is written as 'g/cm^3'. This is how many grams each centimetre cube of the material weighs.

Remember

Copy and complete the sentences below using these words:

> **volume**   **divided**   **hard**

In **h**_____ materials, the particles hold on to each other tightly.

Density is calculated as mass **d**_____ by **v**_____.

You can use this sum to work out density:

Density of material = Mass of the object ÷ Volume of the object

Questions

3 Which object is heavier, a key or a wooden desk?

4 Which object is bigger, a key or a desk?

5 If the desk was the same size as the key, which would be heavier?

6 Use the equation above and a calculator to complete this table.

Object	Material	Mass	Volume	Density (mass divided by volume)
key	steel	40 g	5 cm^3	_____ g/cm^3
fishing weight	lead	20 g	2 cm^3	_____ g/cm^3
wood block	wood	100 g	200 cm^3	_____ g/cm^3
hammer	steel	800 g	100 cm^3	_____ g/cm^3
wooden pencil	wood	30 g	60 cm^3	_____ g/cm^3

Expansion

Key words

contract   When a material gets smaller as it gets colder

expand, expansion   When a material gets bigger as it gets hotter

friction   A force that tries to stop movement

thermometer   A device to measure temperature. There are lots of different types. Some are glass and break easily

When materials get hot, they get bigger. Solids and liquids **expand** only a small amount but with a great deal of force. Gases expand much more.

Designers' problems

Figure 1 Concorde in flight.

This aeroplane flew very fast – so fast that **friction** made the outer skin get very hot. This made the outside of the aircraft expand by 25 cm – but the inside stayed the same size. The inside did not get hot. This caused huge problems in designing the aircraft.

Thermometers

Figure 2 An alcohol thermometer.

When the **thermometer** is heated, the coloured liquid expands up the narrow tube above the bulb. The tube is narrow so a small change in temperature makes a big difference to the level in the tube.

Up, up and away

Figure 3 A gathering of hot air balloons.

Hot air balloons are simple things. They have a gas burner, a big bag to catch the hot air and a basket. When air is hot it expands a great deal. This makes it lighter for its size than the normal air around it. Because it is lighter for its size, it will float up in the normal air.

Ice is the odd one out

Figure 4 Because water expands as it freezes ... icebergs float on top of the sea.

Figure 5 Because water expands as it freezes ... the ice has swelled up inside these water pipes and made cracks in the metal.

Nearly all solids expand when they melt and **contract** when they solidify. But the ice/water change is different.

Ice cubes always float in a glass of water. They must be less heavy for their size than the water round them. Water must expand when it freezes. If you look at an ice cube tray you can see that the level has risen up in each square of the tray.

1 Copy the diagram of the simple water thermometer.

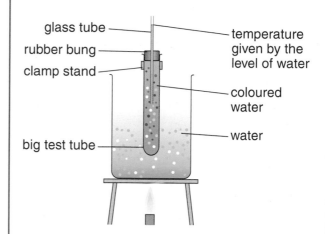

glass tube

rubber bung

clamp stand

temperature given by the level of water

coloured water

water

big test tube

2 Copy and complete this sentence.

When the water in the beaker is heated, the coloured water rises up the glass tube because ...

Remember

Copy and complete the sentences using these words:

solids   same   cool   expand   lot

Nearly all materials **e**_____ on heating and contract when they **c**___. But their mass stays the **s**____.

Gases expand a **l**___ more than **s**_____ and liquids.

Stretchy and bendy

flexible   Bends easily without breaking
inflates   Blows up, fills with air
rigid   Does not bend easily
squashable   Can be made into a smaller volume. The proper scientific word is compressible

Solid particles are in a **rigid** arrangement. Liquid particles are in a crowded jumble. Gas particles whiz about apart from each other. This can be used to explain the physical properties of materials.

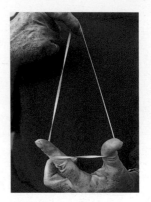

Figure 3 Rubber is stretchy. The particles in rubber are folded up like a zigzag. When the rubber is pulled, the zigzag particles straighten out without breaking

Hitting the water

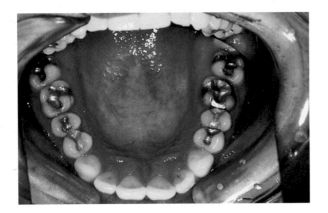

Figure 1 If the fillings were harder than the tooth enamel, they would break the surrounding teeth. Dentists use gold to replace teeth because it has the right hardness.

Figure 4 Children playing in a ball pond

If you dive into a pool and do a 'belly flop', it hurts. But climb down the ladder and the liquid water is soft, not hard.

Particles in a liquid are like the pattern in a children's ball pond.

Step into the ball pond and you can sink right through it. But if you 'belly flop' into the ball pond from high up, there is no time for the particles to push apart before they stop your fall. Ouch! That's why a belly flop into water hurts.

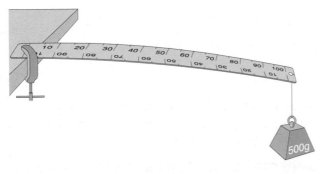

Figure 2 Wood is **flexible**. The particles in wood are long and thin so they bend without breaking.

Questions

1 Draw a strip cartoon showing a 'belly flop' into a ball pond. Add speech bubbles to it. Explain what has happened using scientific words.

A soft landing

Figure 5 A pole-vaulter from 1933 (top). A modern pole-vaulter (bottom).

Years ago, pole-vaulters practised by landing in soft sand. Now they use a modern 'crash mat'. A crash mat is full of air and that absorbs the energy of the pole-vaulter.

Gases are the most **squashable** of all materials. The particles in air are separated from each other. They whiz about very quickly. If a pole-vaulter lands on the crash mat, the air particles get pushed closer together making the soft landing.

An air bag in a car does a similar job during a car crash.

Questions

2 Turn to your partner and explain how safety air bags in cars work. Use these ideas:
- Compressed air is in a small gas bottle inside the steering wheel.
- An electric circuit senses a crash.
- The air bag **inflates** rapidly.
- It stops the driver's head hitting anything hard.

Remember

Copy these sentences and learn the ideas.

Solid materials stay in one shape. They can be broken up or bent by a force, but they stay the same size.

Liquids go into the shape of the container into which they are poured. But their size (volume) stays the same.

Gases can be squashed into a smaller size and shape. They will also spread out to fill all of a space.

Always moving and mixing

Figure 1 The people standing at the carnival take the shape of the space behind the fences

Liquids fill up whatever shape of space there is. But the particles do not stand still. They move past each other.

Figure 2 The dancers at the carnival spread out into the space available

In gases, the particles are far apart and are moving about quickly. Gases spread to take up all the space in the container. The gas particles move about everywhere. They sometimes bump into each other or bounce back from the walls. The force of the particles bumping into the walls is the pressure inside the gas.

Brownian motion

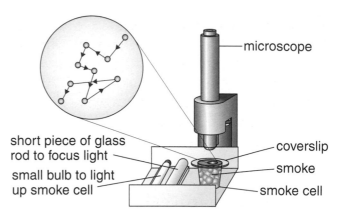

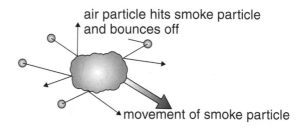

Figure 3 Brownian motion in smoke particles

Particles in a gas or liquid move about randomly. This is called **Brownian motion**. The gas particles are too small to see. But if there are some specks of smoke in the gas, the gas particles will make the bigger smoke particles jiggle about as they hit them. You can see the movement of the smoke particles with a microscope.

Diffusion

Figure 4 You can show diffusion in a liquid using blackcurrant syrup

Particles in liquids and gases move about all the time.

If you carefully pour blackcurrant syrup into a glass of still water, it forms a layer of syrup at the bottom. If you leave it for the rest of the day, the random movements of the liquid particles mix the syrup with the water. This is called **diffusion**. Diffusion only happens in liquids and gases.

A new smell spreads out

Figure 5 The dancers from the carnival smell the deodorant at different times as it diffuses across the room

Liz was in the carnival procession. She was changing for the evening. She sprayed a new deodorant all over herself.

Sahera was next to her. She noticed the new perfume first and wanted to know what it was. It smelt really good.

Then Jalminder, who was changing next to Sahera, noticed the smell as well and wanted to know the brand name.

Finally Julia on the far side of the changing room asked where she could get some.

Questions

1 Draw a picture of how a mug of sand looks when it is poured out on to the floor.

2 Explain what would have happened if the mug had contained milk.

3 Read the part about the deodorant. What is the name of the process that spreads the smell?

4 Draw a particles diagram to show how the perfume smell spreads through the air.

Remember

Copy and complete the sentences using these words:

**smell   diffusion   mix   flow
Brownian motion**

Liquids and gases are fluid. This means they **f____**.

The movement of the particles in gases and liquids is called **B_____ m_____**.

Fluids will also **m_____** together. The process is called **d_____**. This is how a **s_____** spreads.

Watching changes

Have you ever seen a **video** running backwards? Sometimes you make a mistake and think it looks real. Clever people say we can only tell that time is passing because everything in the world is getting more mixed together.

If you leave a bucket of **water** out in the garden, it doesn't stay as just a bucket of water for very long. You don't have to do anything to it.

The water **evaporates** and makes a **mixture** with the **air**.

Things fall into the water and dissolve to make a **solution.** When the water evaporates and more rain falls, the solution becomes more concentrated.

Particles of dust from weathered **rock**, and bits of **soil** blow into the bucket.

Little **organisms** like algae and bacteria arrive on the soil particles and live on the salts in the water. Soon the water begins to look green as lots of algae and bacteria grow in it.

Plants like **grass** or moss may take root near the moisture.

With things to eat in the water and near the water, **insects** and snails will use the bucket as somewhere to live. These animals will **filter** the living things out of the water and eat them.

Then larger animals – maybe even a **frog** – will turn up to eat the smaller creatures.

Even the **metal** bucket will be affected by the air and water. If it is iron, it will **rust**. It changes **colour** and the surface becomes **flaky**. This makes it easier for the moss to grow.

If you took a video of these events and ran it backwards, nobody would think it was running forwards.

Things mix together and change naturally as time goes by. You can see time has gone by because things get more and more mixed together.

Questions

1   When you read the passage, does it make pictures appear in your head like a video clip? That's understanding!

Draw one of the pictures you saw in your head.

2   Here is a list of words. Copy them down one side of a page. Write their meanings next to them.

video

water

evaporates

mixture

air

solution

rock

soil

organisms

grass

insects

filter

frog

metal

rust

colour

flaky

Finishing off!

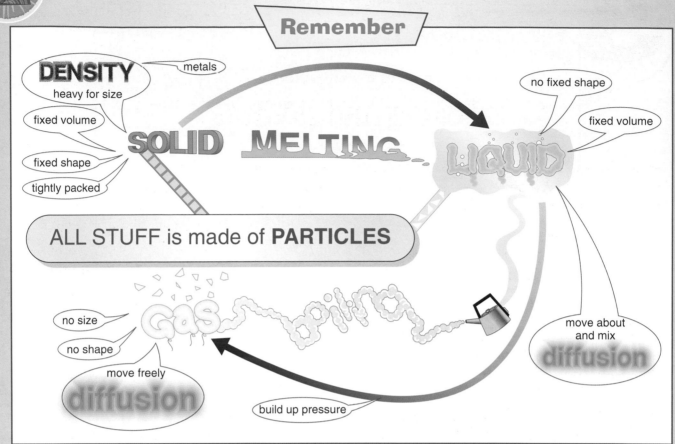

Remember

DENSITY — metals
heavy for size
fixed volume
fixed shape
tightly packed

SOLID   MELTING   LIQUID

no fixed shape
fixed volume

ALL STUFF is made of PARTICLES

Gas boiling

no size
no shape
move freely
diffusion

build up pressure

move about and mix
diffusion

Questions

1 Take a new page in your exercise book. Make a list of all the Key Words from the boxes in this chapter down the side. Take two lines per word. Try to write the meaning of each word without looking. Then go back and fill in any you did not know or got wrong.

2 a) Why do we use glass for windows?

   b) Why do we use rubber for tyres?

   c) Why do we use wool for clothes?

   d) Why do we use steel for hammers?

3 Make a big picture of 'Carnival People' (like on page 14) but make yours a bit different. Put labels on it to explain why the people are like the particles in solids, liquids and gases.

Web sites to visit:

Solids, liquids, gases
http://www.dist214.k12.il.us/users/asanders/slg.html

Energy and fuels

Starter Activity
People and potatoes

People need energy to grow, to move and to keep warm. We get our energy from food. We can store food to use later.

Plants need energy to grow. They get their energy from the Sun. Their green leaves collect energy from the Sun.

Potato plants store energy in the thick parts of their roots. These are the potatoes that we eat. They are a kind of fuel for our bodies. The green parts of the plant die in winter. The potato plant will use this store of energy to help it grow again in spring.

Questions

Copy and complete these sentences. Use these words:

food   energy   leaves   roots   Sun

1   We need **e_____** to grow and move and keep warm.

2   A plant uses its green **l_____** to collect energy from the **S__**.

3   A potato plant stores energy in its **r____**.

4   Our bodies need a fuel. We call it **f__**.

Temperature changes

Figure 1

Key words

degree Celsius (°C)   A unit used to measure temperature

temperature   A measure of how hot or cold something is

thermometer   An instrument used to measure temperature

unit   A scale of measurement

variable   Something which can change

'Hungry?' said Chris.

'You bet,' I said.

'OK, but first we must let the oven warm up, then the pizza will start to cook.'

'How long will that be?' I asked.

'We must wait a few minutes for the oven to get to 180 °C. Then it will be hot enough to put the pizza in. It will need to cook for 20 minutes.'

Temperature is a measure of how hot something is. It is something that changes. We say it is a **variable**. We use a **thermometer** to measure temperature.

When we measure anything we must always give the **unit** as well as the number. When we measure length, we measure it in metres. We say that a line is 3 metres (3 m) long. In this case, the number is 3 and the unit is metres.

With temperature, we say the temperature of the oven is 180 **degrees Celsius** (180 °C). The number is 180 and the unit is degrees Celsius (°C).

Questions

1 Name the unit we use to measure temperature.

2 What do we call a quantity which changes?

3 When we heat something, what happens to its temperature?

Measuring temperature

We use thermometers to measure temperature. Most thermometers are made from a glass tube with a bulb at one end. There is a liquid in the bulb. This is usually alcohol or mercury. The mercury is a silver colour. The alcohol can be red or blue.

As the temperature of the liquid in the bulb increases, the liquid expands. It moves up the inside of the tube. The outside of the tube has marks and numbers on it. These are called a scale. This thermometer is measuring a temperature of 30 °C.

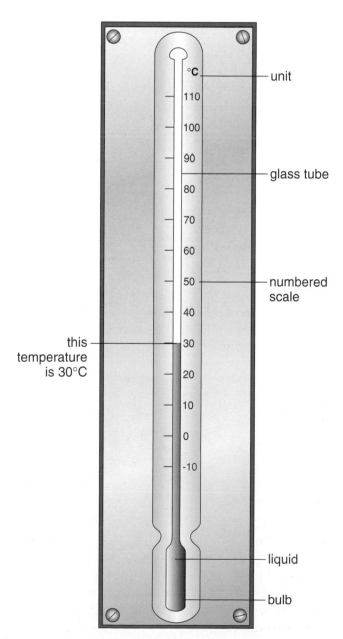

°C — unit

110
100
90   — glass tube
80
70
60
50   — numbered scale
40
this ——   30
temperature   20
is 30°C
                      10
                      0
                      -10

liquid

bulb

Figure 2 A liquid thermometer. This thermometer reads 30 °C.

Questions

4 Draw a thermometer in your book. Go from 0 °C to 100 °C. Use 1 cm to equal 10 °C.

5 Mark today's temperature on your scale.

Remember

Copy and complete the sentences. Use these words:

**degree Celsius   bulb   scale   hot
mercury   variable   temperature
thermometer**

Temperature is a measure of how **h**____ something is. We use a **t**____ to measure it. The unit of temperature is the **d**_____ **C**_____.The thermometer has a glass **b**____ with alcohol or **m**_____ in it. When the **t**____ changes, the liquid moves along the **s**_____ on the thermometer. A quantity which changes is called a **v**__.

Energy from the Sun

We get energy from the Sun. It gives us heat and light. Plants and solar cells can use this energy resource.

Figure 1 Plant leaves have large flat surfaces. The leaves absorb light and use it to make food. This is called **photosynthesis**. Plants need energy to grow.

Figure 2 Plants provide the energy resources for animals. Cows eat grass. It gives them energy to keep their bodies warm, to grow and to move.

Figure 3 Other plants provide us with an energy resource. Photosynthesis changed the energy from the Sun into food energy. The apple is a source of food energy.

Figure 4 Trees use energy from the light of the Sun to grow. We can use the trees as a fuel to keep us warm. Fuel made from material that has been alive is called a **biomass** energy resource.

Figure 5 Trees and other plants die and fall over. In some places like forests and swamps, layers of them build up. Some might get buried by mud and sand.

Figure 6 Coal is formed from layers of plants that died millions of years ago. This coal mine is deep underground. The miner is digging out the coal.

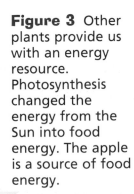

Figure 7 Sometimes you can still find signs of the old plants in the coal. This is a fossil of a leaf. It grew millions of years ago, long before the dinosaurs. Coal is a **fossil fuel**.

Figure 8 There are **solar cells** on the roof of this house. The cells transform light energy from the Sun into electricity. They only generate energy when the Sun is shining. They can charge up batteries so that we can use the energy later.

Figure 9 The heat energy from the Sun makes the winds blow. When the wind blows, these generators convert energy from the wind to electricity.

Key words

biomass   A fuel made from material that has been alive, for example wood.

fossil fuel   A fuel made from plants and animals which lived millions of years ago.

photosynthesis   Process in which plants make their own food using light energy.

solar cell   A device which changes light energy into electrical energy.

Questions

Copy and complete these sentences using the key words to help you.

1 a) Plants make their own food from sunlight. This is called **p**_____.
   b) Fuel made from living material is called **b**_____.
   c) A fuel made from living material that died millions of years ago is called a **f**_____ fuel.
   d) To transform the energy from the Sun into electricity we use a **s**_____ cell.

2 Make a list of different energy resources. Here are two to get you started: coal, food.

Remember

Photo means to do with light.

Bio means to do with life.

Solar means to do with the Sun.

Write down any other words you can think of which begin with:
a) Photo
b) Bio
c) Solar

Electricity: the true cost

Renewable and non-renewable

We all like the good things we can do with electricity: watch TV, use computers, play electronic games. We use electricity to heat and light our homes.

Electricity is generated at power stations. They burn a lot of fuel, usually coal, oil or gas. These fuels come from under the ground. They were formed millions of years ago. One day they will all be used up. They cannot be replaced. We say they are **non-renewable**.

When these fuels burn, they send harmful gases into the air. This causes pollution.

Some energy resources are **renewable**. They will not run out. As long as the the Sun shines, we will always have winds. We can use the energy in the wind to drive a wind generator. Making electricity this way does not cause pollution.

We have a choice. Keep on using electricity the way we do now and it will run out. Or stop using electricity. Or use more renewable resources. Some of the choices are shown below.

Energy resource	Renewable or non-renewable	Pollution level	Advantages
Coal is a **fossil fuel**. It was made from plants that were buried millions of years ago. At the power station, coal is burned which boils water to make steam. The steam turns the generators to make electricity.	Non-renewable	Very high	There is a lot of coal still in the ground. It is cheap to use.
Gas is a fossil fuel. It was made from the bodies of animals that died millions of years ago. The burning gas turns the generators in a power station.	Non-renewable	High	Cheap to use in large and medium-sized power stations.

Energy resource	Renewable or non-renewable	Pollution level	Advantages
Oil is another fossil fuel. Oil is burned in a power station. The steam turns generators to produce electricity.	Non-renewable	Very high	Quite cheap to use in medium-sized power stations.
Biomass is waste material from plants and animals. It includes sewage. Biomass is burned in a power station. Like the other fuels it produces steam to drive the electricity generators.	Renewable	High. But if we keep growing new plants then a lot of the pollution is taken out of the air.	If we grow as many plants as we burn, biomass fuel need never run out.
Wind energy uses the energy of moving air. It is used to turn wind generators.	Renewable	Low, but some people think wind generators spoil the peace of the countryside.	There is no burning involved. Wind will blow for billions of years.
Sunlight or solar energy direct from the Sun	Renewable	Very low – they don't produce any pollution	Energy from the Sun will last billions of years. There is no burning involved.

Electricity: the true cost continued

Fossil fuels produce pollution

When fossil fuels burn, they produce pollution. In cities they can create **smog**. This smoky fog is very bad for you if you breathe it.

Burning fossil fuels makes **acid rain**. Acid rain causes a lot of damage. It kills trees and even fish in lakes. It damages the bricks and stones of buildings.

When we burn fossil fuels we make a gas called carbon dioxide. This gas goes into the air. Carbon dioxide keeps the Earth warm. Burning more fuels will make the Earth even warmer. It will change our climate. It will cause **global climate change** with more deserts and more stormy weather.

Questions

1 Name two good things we get from fossil fuels.

2 Name two bad things we get from fossil fuels.

Fossil fuels will not last forever

Fossil fuels were made from dead plants and animals millions of years ago. We cannot make any more. They are non-renewable. We have used up most of them already. Look at Figure 1 to see how long they will last.

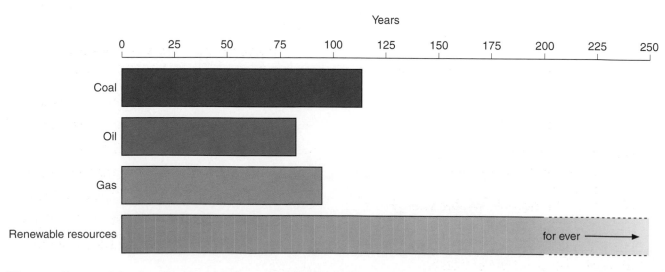

Figure 1 Fossil fuels will not last forever. Renewable resources will.

Energy source for generating electricity	Advantage	Disadvantage
Coal	Cheap to run, cheap to build	Acid rain and global warming
Oil	Cheap to run, cheap to start up	Acid rain and global warming
Gas	Very cheap to run, very quick to start up	Global warming
Nuclear	No burning, so no acid rain or global warming	Radioactive waste is dangerous. Accidents can be very dangerous
Hydro-electric	No fuel costs. Quick to start up. Lakes can also be used for leisure.	Needs hilly country and lots of rain
Wind	No fuel costs. Can be built any size	Takes up a lot of space. Some think the generators are ugly. The supply is unreliable
Wave	No fuel costs	Very expensive to build. Unreliable supply
Tidal	Regular supply four times a day. Low running costs	Very expensive to build. Destroys habitats. Not many suitable locations
Electricity from solar energy	Can be installed anywhere. Small generators possible. No running costs	Very expensive. Only works during the day
Heat from solar energy	No fuel costs. Useful way of heating water in hot countries	Unreliable in United Kingdom. Can be used to heat water, but not generate electricity

Table 1 Comparing energy sources.

Making the right choice

We can generate electricity from many sources. There is no perfect choice. Look at the table above. It compares the different methods for:

- how much they cost to build and run
- how reliable the supply would be
- how much they damage the environment.

Questions

3 Look back at pages 34 and 35.
   a) List all the renewable energy resources.
   b) List all the non-renewable energy resources.

4 What are the disadvantages of using
   a) coal   b) wind generators?

Remember

Copy and complete the sentences. Use these words:

**resources   non-renewable
renewable   generate   fossil**

Oil, coal, gas, biomass, wind, moving water and sunlight are all energy **r**_____. We can use them to **g**____ electricity. Oil, coal and gas are **f**____ fuels. They were made millions of years ago. They cannot be replaced. They are **n**____. Biomass, wind, water and sunlight are all **r**____ energy resources. They will not run out.

Sunshine

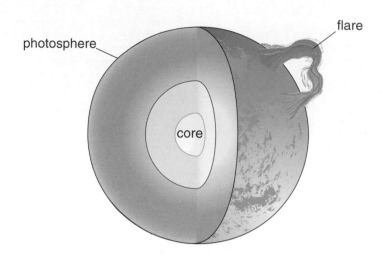

Where does our energy come from? Most of it comes from the Sun.

The Sun is our nearest star. It is at the centre of our Solar System. Long ago some people used to worship the Sun. It was their god. Today we still like the Sun. We feel much happier on a sunny day. Try to imagine what it would be like if the Sun was switched off! What would happen to life on Earth?

The Sun is just like billions of other stars in the Universe. But how big is it? What is it made of? Where does it get its energy from? How long will it last?

The Sun has a very large mass. It is made from two gases, hydrogen and helium. Sunshine is made by a reaction called nuclear fusion. The reactions in the Sun are like those in a nuclear bomb. The hydrogen particles are smashed into each other. They join together to form helium particles. When this happens, small amounts of the mass of the hydrogen are converted directly into a very large amount of energy.

Every second the Sun loses 4 million tonnes of its mass as energy. We get a small part of this energy. It is the Earth's main energy source. It is enough to keep us alive.

The Sun sends us this energy. We use its heat and light. It comes from its outer surface, the part we can see. This part is called the photosphere. The temperature on the surface of the Sun is about 6000 °C. Deep in the centre of the Sun is the **core**. There the temperature is about 15 million °C!

The Sun does not burn like a fire. If it did it would have burnt out in about 50 years. The Sun has been there for about 10 billion years. There is enough energy left to last us for 20 billion years.

Sunspots and flares

Sunspots are darker spots that appear on the surface of the Sun about every 11 years. They are a little cooler that the rest of the photosphere. They cause bright **flares**. These send out charged particles. When these reach the Earth, they can interfere with TV and radio communications.

Solar eclipse

A solar eclipse is when the Moon passes in front of the Sun. Then you can see a bright red region called the chromosphere. This is a layer of gas about 100 km thick. Sometimes large glowing gas jets shoot out from the chromosphere. They shoot into space to a height of over 300 000 km.

When the Moon passes in front of the Sun and covers up the bright central part, you can see the **corona**. This is the outer layer of the Sun beyond the chromosphere and you can only see it during an eclipse.

A total eclipse is when the Moon completely covers up the Sun. Then it goes dark, the temperature drops and animals think it is night time. There was a total eclipse of the Sun in August 1999. It was seen in Devon and Cornwall.

Warning: Never look directly at the Sun and never look at it with a telescope or binoculars. Your eyes will be permanently damaged.

Questions

1 Why do you think people used to worship the sun?

2 Imagine that you lived 1000 years ago. The dark shadow of the Moon begins to creep across the surface of the Sun. You don't know about solar eclipses. Write a diary entry for that day. Write about how you and your family felt. Begin it like this:

"Today a very strange thing happened."

Fuels

Key words

joule   Unit for measuring energy
megajoule   One million joules

Most cars use petrol or diesel as their fuel. Petrol comes from oil. That means it is a fossil fuel. Diesel is also a fossil fuel. Some cars can use alcohol. Some can use liquid petroleum gas (LPG). All these engines have spark plugs except for the diesel engines.

Heat engines

In a car engine, air and a little bit of fuel (petrol) are mixed. When the spark plug fires, it sets off a small explosion. The explosion pushes the piston down. This turns the crankshaft which makes the wheels turn. Only a small amount of fuel burns at each explosion. There are lots of explosions, one after the other.

Questions

1   Name four fuels which can be used in engines.
2   Which two fuels are the most common?
3   What is the fuel mixed with?

The energy value of fuels

Different fuels give off different amounts of heat energy. They have different energy values.

We measure the energy value of different fuels by burning them and seeing how much heat they give off. We can do an experiment like this:

spark plug

the explosions make the engine HOT

cylinder

explosion of fuel and air

the explosions do work to move the piston

piston

the up and down movement of the pistons turn the crankshaft round. The crankshaft is connected to the gearbox and to the wheels

explosions inside a car's engine make its wheels go round

Figure 1 What happens inside a car engine.

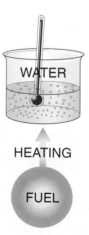

Figure 2 Measuring the energy value of a fuel.

40

To make it a fair test we must:

- use the same amount of fuel each time

- make the fuel heat the same amount of water

- make sure the water starts at the same temperature

A fuel with a high energy value will give out more heat. The water at the end of the experiment will get very hot. A fuel with a low energy value will give out less heat so the water temperature will be lower.

Measuring energy values of fuels

We measure energy in **joules** or J for short. Mega means a million of something. A joule is a very small unit so we often use **megajoules** instead.

We measure the amount or mass of the fuel in grams or kilograms
(1 kilogram = 1000 grams).

The energy value of coal is 35 megajoules per kilogram (35 MJ/kg). That means that
1 kilogram of coal provides 35 megajoules of energy when it burns.

The energy values of some fuels are shown in Table 1.

Fuel	Energy value in megajoules per kilogram
hydrogen	140
methane	52
petrol	48
coal	35
butter	34
sugar	17
wood	13

Table 1 Comparing the energy value of different fuels.

Foods have energy values too! Food is a fuel for our bodies. It gives our bodies energy. The energy value of food is often printed on the label. A small chocolate cream egg will give you about 4 megajoules (4 MJ) of energy.

Questions

4   Which fuels in Table 1 can you use for your body?

5   Which fuel has the highest energy value?

6   How many joules are there in a megajoule?

7   Make a bar chart to show the energy values of the different fuels in Table 1. You may use a computer.

Remember

Copy and complete the sentences. Use these words:

**megajoule   joule   kilogram   gram
fair test   energy value**

We measure energy in units called a **j**_____.
One million joules is called one **m**_____. We can compare the **e**_____ **v**_____ of different fuels. We must carry out a **f**_____ **t**_____.
We measure the mass of coal using a unit called a **g**_____. 1000 grams is called a **k**_____.

Finishing off!

Remember

★ We use lots of **energy resources**: oil, coal, gas, biomass, food, wind, waves and sunlight.

★ The Sun provides most of our energy resources. Oil, coal and gas come from the bodies of animals and plants that lived millions of years ago. They stored energy from the Sun when they were alive. Oil, coal and gas are called **fossil fuels**.

★ Fossil fuels are **non-renewable** energy resources. Once we have used them, we cannot use them again.

★ Energy resources like wind, waves and solar energy are **renewable**. Biomass is renewable if we plant as much as we burn. The Sun keeps on renewing these energy resources.

★ In power stations, fuels are burned to make steam. The steam makes turbines turn. This makes the generators go round. They generate electricity.

★ Some fuels produce more energy than others. They have different **energy values**. We measure the energy value of a fuel in megajoules per kilogram of fuel.

★ Fossil fuels have a high energy value.

Questions

1 Take a new page in your exercise book. Make a list of all the Key Words from the boxes in this chapter down the side. Take two lines per word. Try to write the meaning of each word without looking. Then go back and fill in any you did not know or got wrong.

2 a) Name one fuel that power stations can use.
 b) Where does this fuel come from?
 c) What happens to the fuel in the power station?
 d) Name three problems caused by using fuels in power stations.

3 Draw a poster to show:
 a) that our fossil fuels are running out and polluting our air.
 b) that renewable energy resources are better for us.

4 Your grandad says that we will always have fossil fuels. "They will always find more", he says. Explain to him why he is wrong.

Web sites to visit:

Science Across The World – Renewable Energy
    http://www.scienceacross.org/english/the_topics/index.html

CHAPTER 4

Reproduction

Starter Activity
Growing up

This chapter looks at reproduction and how we change as we grow up. All animals and plants produce young, called offspring, that will grow into adults.

Questions

1 The pictures above show some animals and their offspring. Can you match the offspring with the adult? Remember that not all offspring look like small versions of the adults. Some can be quite different. If you can, try and put the correct name for the offspring, for example, cats produce kittens and dogs produce puppies.

2 Put these in the correct order:
   adult, child, baby, teenager

3 Put these stages for a plant in the correct order:
   seed   flower
   pollination   germination

43

Starting a new life

Being a parent is a big responsibility. Babies have to be looked after, fed and changed. Making sure that they are warm and safe is a full time job. A new life begins when a **sperm cell** from the father joins with an **egg cell** from the mother. This is called **fertilisation**. In mammals it happens inside the female's body.

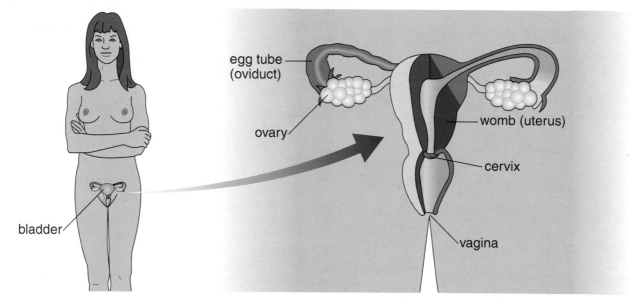

egg tube (oviduct)

ovary

womb (uterus)

cervix

bladder

vagina

Figure 1 The female reproductive system.

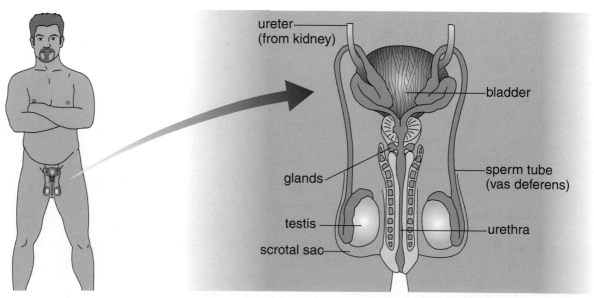

ureter (from kidney)

bladder

glands

sperm tube (vas deferens)

testis

urethra

scrotal sac

Figure 2 The male reproductive system.

Making sperm and egg cells

Egg cells are made inside a woman's **ovaries**. One egg is released each month. The egg cell passes down the egg tube or oviduct. If the egg meets and joins with a sperm cell, fertilisation takes place. The fertilised egg enters the womb (uterus) and attaches itself to the wall of the womb. It may then divide and grow into a baby. This takes about nine months.

Sperm cells are made in the man's **testes**. Sperm cells are very sensitive to temperature. A man's body temperature is too high for sperm cells so the testes hang outside the body in a sac of skin, the scrotal sac or scrotum. When sperm cells are produced, they pass through the sperm tube or vas deferens. Fluids are added which keep the sperm cells alive. The sperm and the fluid together are known as semen.

Remember

Match the following words to their meanings. Try doing this in small groups and saying aloud the words and meanings.

Words	Meanings
1 A sperm cell is	where sperm cells are made.
2 An egg cell is	the joining of a sperm and egg cell.
3 The testes are	the female sex cell.
4 Fertilisation is	the male sex cell.
5 The scrotum is	a bag of skin that hangs outside the man's body.

Questions

1 Copy and complete the table into your exercise book by filling in the 'male or female or both' column.

Name	Male or female or both	What job does it do
oviduct		carries the egg from the ovary to the womb
vas deferens (sperm duct)		carries the sperm from the testes
bladder		stores urine
scrotal sac		where sperm are made
womb (uterus)		where the fertilised egg grows into a baby

2 Where are the sperm produced in men?

3 Where are the eggs produced in women?

4 Imagine having to look after something very fragile all day long, like an uncooked egg. This is like caring for a baby. How would you protect it?
   a) on the way to school? b) in lessons?
   c) during break? d) at lunch time?
   You cannot give your egg to someone else to look after!

Fertilisation

Key words

penis Sperm are ejected out through the penis

vagina Sperm are deposited in the vagina

womb (uterus) Where the fertilised egg develops into a baby

Making love is not just about having babies. Men and women will make love for pleasure and to show their love and commitment.

While making love the man becomes excited and his **penis** becomes stiff or erect. This happens because it fills with blood. When a woman becomes excited she produces a fluid that coats the **vagina** and the entrance to the vagina. This makes it easier for the man's penis to enter the vagina and move in and out. Eventually the sperm are pumped into the vagina in the semen as the man ejaculates.

Sexual intercourse

When people have sexual intercourse or 'make love' it means that the egg and sperm can come into contact with each other.

During sexual intercourse the man's penis becomes stiff. This is due to blood flowing into the penis.

When the woman becomes excited she produces a fluid in the vagina.

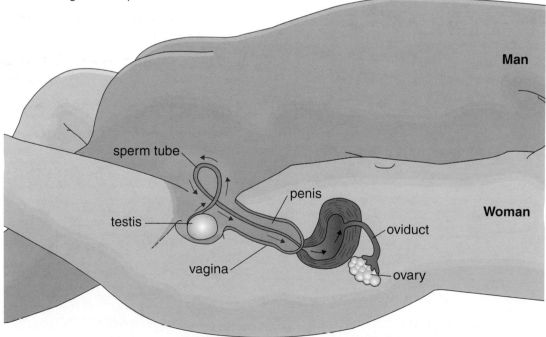

The penis can now slip into the vagina. It is moved backwards and forwards to give the man and woman feelings of pleasure.

Eventually the sperms are pumped from the testis through the penis into the vagina.

Figure 1 The position of the male and the female during sexual intercourse.

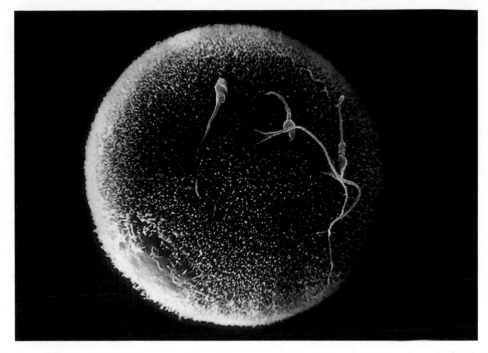

Figure 2 The egg is many times larger than the sperm.

Questions

1 At what age do you think a person is ready to have sex? Explain your answer.

The sperm then swim from the vagina into the **womb** and reach the oviduct. If there is an egg in the oviduct or womb, it could be fertilised by a sperm and the woman will become pregnant. The fertilised egg will travel down the oviduct and attach itself to the wall of the womb. It will then grow into a baby.

Remember

Use these words to copy and complete the sentences below:

**inside fertilisation intercourse
womb swim pregnant**

Sexual **i**_____ can make a woman **p**_____. Sperm cells can **s**_____ quite a long way **i**_____ a woman's body. **F**_____ can take place in the oviduct or the **w**____.

Questions

2 At what age do you think a person is ready to be a parent? Explain your answer.

3 What qualities do you think a parent should have?

Growing in the womb

foetus   The name given to a baby growing inside the mother's womb

placenta   A round disc shaped organ that transfers things from the mother to the baby and from the baby to the mother

umbilical cord   A tube that connects the baby to the placenta

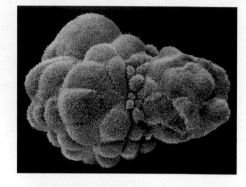

b) 6 days

Once a fertilised egg attaches to the wall of the womb, it begins to grow and develop into a baby. At first it is just a ball of cells. The cells divide just like the ones we saw on pages 6 and 7. After about 4 weeks it is possible to see the head of the baby beginning to develop. Tiny stumps will develop into the legs and arms. At this stage the baby is called a **foetus**.

Look at the photos that show you how the baby develops.

c) 28 days

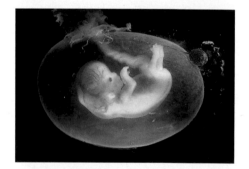

d) 8 weeks

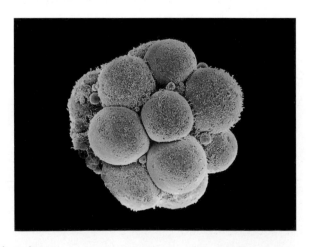

a) 4 days

Figure 1 The stages of development of a baby.

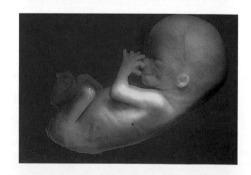

e) 15 weeks

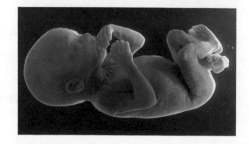

f) 23 weeks

As the baby grows it needs food and oxygen. It needs protection against germs and needs to get rid of waste products. The **placenta** does all these things. It grows on the surface of the womb. It is like a round disc that is connected to the baby by the **umbilical cord**. The placenta has lots of tiny thin blood vessels. They let the oxygen and chemicals that the baby needs (for energy and growth) pass from the mother's bloodstream into the baby's bloodstream. Any waste that the baby produces passes down the umbilical cord and across to the mother's bloodstream for the mother to get rid of.

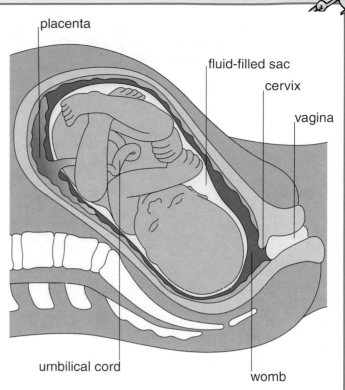

Figure 2 A baby in its mother's womb.

Questions

1   How does the growing baby get a supply of food and oxygen?

2   Why does the growing baby need the mother to eat properly during pregnancy?

3   How does the baby get rid of waste products?

While it is in the mother's body, the baby lives inside a fluid-filled sac. This acts like a cushion and protects the baby from small knocks and bumps.

The placenta can stop some harmful substances and some bacteria from passing into the baby but it cannot stop everything. For example, alcohol can pass into the baby, which can harm the baby as it grows. Harmful chemicals in cigarette smoke can also pass into the baby's bloodstream and can cause problems as it grows.

Questions

4   The baby lives inside a fluid-filled sac until it is ready to be born. How does this protect the baby?

5   Why are pregnant women advised not to smoke or drink during pregnancy?

Remember

Copy and complete the paragraph below using the words in the list. A word may be used more than once!

**blood   umbilical cord   fertilised
mother's   baby's   placenta
oxygen   baby   food**

The **f**_____ egg grows and divides inside the **m**_____ womb. The mother's **b**____ stream and the **b**_____ bloodstream are separate. The baby needs **f**_____ and **o**_____. The **p**_____ is the organ that allows this to happen. The baby is connected to the **p**_____ by the **u**_____ **c**____.

Growing up is hard to do

Puberty

As you grow into an adult, things will happen to you. They won't all happen at the same time to everyone. This is normal. When you change from being a child to an adult you go through a stage called **puberty**. Puberty can be a difficult time, but it's nothing to worry about. We also call this time **adolescence**.

Question

1   Describe the changes that you can see in Figure 1 as a boy and a girl change from an adolescent to an adult.

Menstruation

Once a girl reaches adolescence, she begins to have periods. This is what we call **menstruation**. As we have found out, women produce an egg once a month. What happens if the egg is not fertilised? Once an egg is released, the wall of the womb thickens. The lining of the womb has lots of blood vessels. If a fertilised egg does not reach the womb and attach to the lining, the body knows that the lining is not needed. The blood-filled lining breaks down and is passed out of the body through the vagina, with a small amount of blood.

For some young girls periods may be irregular. As they grow older the periods should settle down and happen once every 28–30 days. The egg is released around day 14. The first day of bleeding in a woman is day 1 of their period.

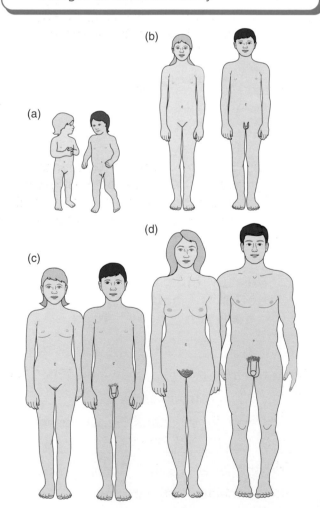

Figure 1 These pictures show some of the changes that take place when you grow up.

During puberty what happens to ...	Boys	Girls
my body size?	Your body begins to grow faster. Your shoulders will broaden. You will be able to see more defined muscles.	Your body begins to grow faster. You will begin to get curves as your body deposits fat on your hips, buttocks and thighs.
my hair	The hair on your head could become greasier. You will begin to grow body hair under your arms and on your chest, arms and legs. Hair will grow around your penis (pubic hair). You will also begin to grow facial hair.	The hair on your head could become greasier. You will begin to grow body hair, for example under your arms. Hair will grow around your vagina (pubic hair).
my voice?	Your voice will become deeper and your larynx (Adam's Apple) gets larger.	Your voice won't change much.
my skin?	You could develop 'spots' or mild acne. If it gets bad see your chemist or doctor.	You could develop 'spots' or mild acne. If it gets bad see your chemist or doctor.
my reproductive organs?	Your testes will grow larger and start producing sperm. Your penis will grow larger and may get slightly darker.	You will begin to grow breasts (mammary glands). Your ovaries will begin to produce eggs. You will start to menstruate (have periods).

Table 1 Changes that happen during puberty. Many of these are controlled by hormones.

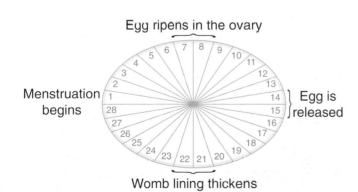

Figure 2 The stages in the menstrual cycle

Girls may begin to have periods at any age from about 9–17 years old. Usually periods start at around the age of 13 or 14. Lots of things can affect exactly when a girl's period will first begin. These things include diet, health, the amount of exercise she does and her weight.

Questions

2 Young girls often try to diet as they are going through puberty. What changes in their bodies might make young girls want to diet and why could it be harmful to them?

Remember

Write a sentence to describe what happens at puberty to the following

★ A boy's voice
★ Body hair on boys and girls
★ Muscles
★ Boys' and girls' skin
★ Boys' and girls' reproductive organs

The problem page

Teenage magazines often have a problem page with an agony aunt or uncle. This is your chance to be an agony aunt or uncle. Read the problems below and try to give good, sensible advice. Write a letter in reply to each of the problems.

Teenage problem 1

Dear problem page

I am a boy about 12 years of age. The problem is that every time I open my mouth, my voice seems to squeak. One minute it's high, the next very low. It's difficult for me to answer questions in class because I think the others will make fun of me. Can you help me and let me know what's going on?

Worried of Wandsworth

Teenage problem 2

Dear problem page

My mother keeps on at me about how often I wash my hair. The trouble is I think it is greasy. It never used to be like this. There is no way that I am going to school with hair like that. She keeps shouting at me in the morning to hurry up in the shower. It wouldn't be so bad but she takes twice as long as me! If I could only give her a reason why I take so long then it wouldn't be so bad. Can you help?

Annoyed of Andover

Teenage problem 3

Dear problem page

It's just not fair! I'm 14 and I haven't had my first period yet. I must be a freak. All my friends say they've had loads. Am I really a freak? Will I ever have a period?

Depressed of Derby

Teenage problem 4

Dear problem page

My mother is pregnant and I am worried. I don't see how a baby can survive inside her. I know that we all need oxygen to live and food to help us grow, including babies! What I don't understand is how the baby will get these if it's inside my mum. Can you please explain what is going on?

Confused of Clacton

Teenage problem 5

Dear problem page

When I have a shower after P.E., I find it difficult because I am beginning to grow some hair under my arms and around my private parts. Is this normal? (I am 12 years of age.) I thought that only adults grew hair on their body. Am I too young for this? My friends point and snigger but am I right that this will also happen to them?

Shy of Sheffield

Teenage problem 6

Dear problem page

My friends have told me that kissing and cuddling can make a girl pregnant. I'm not certain that it does. I know that fertilisation has to take place because I remember hearing something about it in my science lesson. I wasn't listening in class so I didn't hear the rest. I'm too embarrassed to go back and ask my science teacher as she will think I'm an idiot. Can you help me and explain what fertilisation is?

Dreamer of Darlington

Remember

Make a leaflet to answer teenagers' common problems. In a small group decide on some problems and write some answers to the problems. Think of some different problems from the ones on this page.

Finishing off!

Remember

Copy and complete the following paragraph using the words from this list.

ovaries   womb   fertilisation   placenta

When a sperm cell joins with an egg cell it is called **f**_____. This is the start of life. Egg cells are produced in a woman's **o**_____. The egg will travel down the oviduct. If the egg is fertilised, it will attach to the wall of the **w**_____. As the fertilised egg grows in the womb, a round disc-shaped organ called the **p**_____ also grows. This provides oxygen and food for the growing baby.

Copy and complete this paragraph by choosing the correct word from each pair.

In men, sperm cells are produced in the **stomach/testes**. These are found hanging outside the body in the scrotal sacs. The scrotal sacs are outside the body because it is **cooler/warmer** there. Sperm can only develop at cooler temperatures. Sperm are deposited in the vagina during sexual intercourse by the penis. They swim into the **womb/ovary** and up into the oviduct where they can join with an egg. This is called **pollination/fertilisation**.

Questions

1 Take a new page in your exercise book. Make a list of all the Key Words from the boxes in this chapter down the side. Take two lines per word. Try to write the meaning of each word without looking. Then go back and fill in any you did not know or got wrong.

2 At about the age of 12 what do most boys and girls begin to go through?
Answer **P**_____

3 After puberty, girls start to have periods. What is another name for a period?
Answer **M**_____

4 After puberty, the Adam's apple in boys gets larger. What is another name for the Adam's apple?
Answer **L**_____

5 Both boys and girls can suffer from spots during puberty. What is another name for spots?
Answer **A**_____

Web sites to visit:

KidsHealth – answering questions about puberty
http://www.kidshealth.org/kid/grow/puberty.html

Parenthood Web – ultrasound images of foetuses
http://www.parenthood.com/parent_cfmfiles/us.cfm

Solutions

Starter Activity
Filtering

You know about filtering. You have seen it done lots of times. Filtering separates a liquid and a solid.

Operating masks prevent germs from the doctors' mouths getting inside the patient but let air through.

A colander can be used to strain peas. This is like filtering.

A dust mask filters tiny bits of paint to stop them from getting into the lungs, but air can get through.

A filter bed in a sewage works traps bits of solid in the dirty water.

Questions

1 Copy the table below and fill in the spaces.

Name of filter	Substance being left in filter	Substance passing through filter
Operating theatre mask	Germs	
Dust mask		Air
Filter bed	Solid waste	
Colander		Water

2 You can use filtering to separate chalk and water but not salt and water. Why can't you separate salt and water by filtering?

Good solutions

When a solid disappears into a liquid, a mixture called a **solution** is made. The solid that dissolves is called a **solute** and the liquid is a **solvent**.

Concentrate on the job

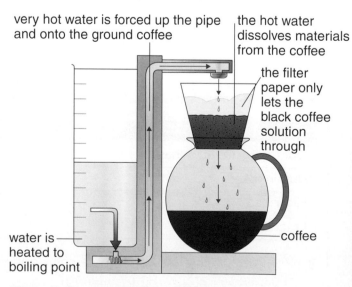

Tom has a Saturday job. But he has made some silly mistakes.

'On my first day I had to make black coffee, but I only know about instant coffee. This was real coffee. I put one spoonful in the cup and added water. It turned out really weak and the coffee bits did not dissolve.

This is what I should have done. Pour boiling water on to the ground coffee and then filter the liquid. The boiling water dissolves the coffee taste particles out of the ground up coffee. The rest stays in the filter. You need to use more ground coffee than you would instant coffee. There is less coffee taste in ground coffee, so the coffee drink would be less strong'.

In Tom's example, the coffee taste particles are the solute and the boiling water is the solvent. The solution is the coffee drink.

When substances dissolve, the solution is **transparent**. It may also be coloured. If it is not transparent, it is not a real solution.

very hot water is forced up the pipe and onto the ground coffee

the hot water dissolves materials from the coffee

the filter paper only lets the black coffee solution through

water is heated to boiling point

coffee

Figure 1 Tom in trouble at the café

Figure 2 How a filter coffee machine works

1 Write down the names of four substances you know that dissolve in water.

2 Next to their names write the colour of the solution they make.

3 Some people like 'weak' tea. How can you tell if tea is weak?

4 If you make a thermos flask of instant coffee, you use much more coffee powder than for a mugful. Explain why.

Figure 3 Making jelly

If you want a substance like jelly to dissolve faster, use hot water and cut the jelly into small pieces. A higher temperature and bigger surface area speed up dissolving.

What is the difference between melting and dissolving?

Dissolving needs two substances – a solute and a solvent. Here are two examples of dissolving:

> Instant coffee and water
> Sugar and water

Melting needs only one substance. Here are two examples of melting:

> Ice cubes on a hot day
> Butter in a frying pan

Remember

Copy and complete the sentences using these words:

solute   solution   solvent   filter

A solid **s_____e** dissolves in a **s_____t** to make a mixture called a **s_____n**.

A solution will pass through a coffee **f_____**.

Picture solutions

Key words

concentrated   Lots of dissolved particles in the solution

concentration   How much substance is dissolved in the solution

dilute   Not many dissolved particles in the solution

dissolved particles   The particles of solute when they are in the solution

saturated   When no more will dissolve

Figure 2 Mata diluting the chemicals she needs to develop her photographs.

Figure 1

Flash! The camera shutter opens for a fraction of a second and the picture is taken.
The film has only a very faint outline of the picture taken.
The film must be developed in a solution.
Then the picture can be seen.

Mata is in charge of processing the pictures. She takes the film out of the camera in the dark. She 'develops' the film in a solution that makes the picture much darker. Mata must add water to dilute the chemicals. If the **concentration** of the solution is wrong, the picture will be ruined. It will turn out to be too light or too dark.

Then the image must be 'fixed.' Mata puts the picture into a solution so that all the light-sensitive material gets **dissolved** out of the film.

The 'fixer' solution needs changing every day because it becomes **saturated** with material from the film.

Questions

1   What does Mata use the developer solution for?

2   Why does Mata have to be careful about diluting the developer solution?

3   What does Mata use fixer solution for?

4   Why does the fixer solution get changed every day?

Complete solutions

Key
Water particles
Salt particles

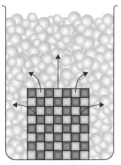

a) The salt goes into the water.

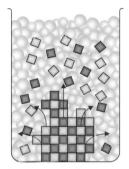

b) The water particles pull the salt particles apart. They mix with the water.

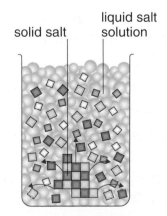

c) When the last particles of salt are pulled apart, the salt disappears.

Figure 3

Figure 3 shows salt dissolving in water. In this example:

- salt is the solute
- water is the solvent
- salty water is the solution.
- The solid gets dissolved layer by layer from the outside in. The solid gets split up into tiny particles and can't be seen anymore.
- A **concentrated** solution has lots of solute particles. A **dilute** solution has few solute particles.

Questions

5 Why can't you see the salt particles in salty water?

6 Draw a particle picture of a dilute solution.

Remember

Copy and complete the sentences using these words:

**solution   dissolved   dilute
concentration   particles**

A **s**_____**n** has dissolved particles in it.

The **c**_____ is the amount of solute **d**_____ in a certain volume of solution. A **d**_____**e** solution has few dissolved **p**_____**s** in it.

Bends & sweets

Solids and **gases** both form solutions. We are used to dissolving solids, but you may not know that gases dissolve as well. These facts may surprise you:

- steel rusts because oxygen dissolves in water.

- fish have gills so they can breathe the dissolved oxygen from water.

- drinks are fizzy because carbon dioxide is dissolved in them.

Deep breathing

When we breathe in air, **oxygen** gets into our blood. But some of the **nitrogen** from the air also dissolves in our body. Normally, having nitrogen in our blood isn't a problem. It just gets carried round and round by the blood.

But the dissolved nitrogen is a danger to scuba divers. As they dive deeper, the **pressure** of the water makes more nitrogen dissolve in their blood. When they come back to surface, the nitrogen has to come out of their blood. If they swim up too fast, the gas comes out of their blood like bubbles in a fizzy drink when the top is undone.

This is called the '**bends**'. It is very painful. Divers can easily die from it.

Questions

1   "Dive too deep or come up too quickly and your blood becomes like a shaken can of cola." Explain why this happens.

2   What effect do the bends have on a diver? Try to find out from books or from the Internet.

Key words

crystals   Perfectly shaped pieces of solid
granulated   The size of particles that sugar is usually bought in
reed   A tall thin plant
vacuum   A very low or even zero air pressure

Sugar from reeds?

Did you know that sugar for sweets, cakes and drinks comes mainly from a tropical **reed** called sugar cane. This grows to 6 metres in height in countries that are hot and wet.
Sugar used to be sold as big solid lumps. Sugar Loaf Mountain in Brazil got its name because it looked like a big lump of sugar.

Making sugar

This is how you turn sugar cane into sugar:

- Shred the cane and wash it with hot water to make a sugar cane juice.

- Heat the juice in a **vacuum**. The water boils at a lower temperature in the vacuum.

- When the solution is saturated, scatter in small crystals of sugar, like icing sugar.

- This causes big **crystals** to grow round the little crystals.

- The big crystals are separated from the syrupy juice and dried.

- The crystals are what we call **granulated** sugar.

Questions

3 What plant does sugar come from?

4 What conditions does sugar need to grow?

5 Why is the cane shredded before the juice is extracted?

6 Why is hot water used?

Salt and water

Questions

1   What is the chemical name for table salt?

2   Why does this process work well in East Africa?

3   What is crystallisation?

Can you get salt from sea water?

Figure 1 You can get salt from sea water. You can see the heaps of salt in this photo.

You cannot drink sea water, but it contains two useful materials: pure water and salt.

Table salt is the chemical called **sodium chloride**. In East Africa they make table salt from sea water. Sea water is pumped into a flat pond and left to **evaporate** in the Sun. The hot Sun helps the water to dry up. The sodium chloride **crystallises**. The table salt can then be sold.

Can you get pure water from sea water?

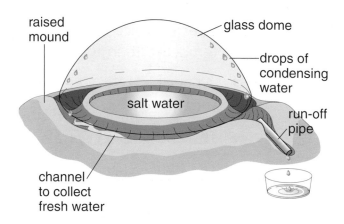

raised mound

glass dome

drops of condensing water

salt water

run-off pipe

channel to collect fresh water

Figure 2 Making pure water by distillation

In a hot dry country, a glass dome over a pool of salt water will make pure water. The Sun evaporates the water. The vapour then **condenses** on the inside of the glass dome. A dome one metre across will produce 4.5 litres of pure water a day.

This process is called **distilling**.

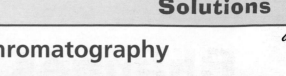

Questions

You can distil water using this apparatus. When you boil salty water, the salt is left behind. The water escapes as steam. If you turned the steam back into water, it would be pure water.

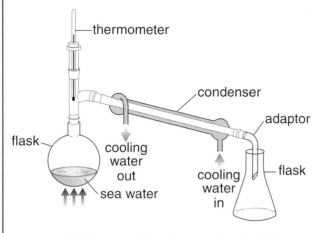

Figure 3 How to distil water in the lab

4 Here are step-by-step instructions to tell someone how to make pure water from sea water. But the instructions are in the wrong order. Copy them out in the right order.

- Boil the water.

- Connect the cooling water pipes.

- Collect the pure water from the condenser.

- Put sea water in the flask.

- Set up the apparatus.

Chromatography

Figure 4 Separating the colours in ink by chromatography.

You will have separated colours like in the picture. This is called chromatography. This works because some colours dissolve more easily than others.

Remember

Copy the table and complete it by matching the words with their **correct** meaning. (*Hint:* Two of them are wrong)

Separation method		Description
distilling		boiling a liquid, then condensing the vapour
evaporating		pieces of solid forming from the liquid mixture
crystallising		liquid escaping from the surface of a solution

Changes of state

Key words

boiling A liquid turning to gas because of strong heating

freezing A liquid turning to solid due to cooling

melting A solid turning to liquid due to heating

Solid, liquid and gas are the three states of matter. One state of matter can change to a different state. For example:

- Going from solid to liquid is called **melting**.

- Going from liquid to gas is called **boiling** or evaporating.

Figure 1 Mandy – the chocoholic!

Breakfast! Mandy is a chocoholic. She likes to start the day with a hot chocolate drink and a piece of cake with chocolate on the top.

Melting

When the chocolate is heated by the hot water, it melts. It changes from chunks to a brown liquid.

The liquid chocolate is spread on the cake. As it cools, it turns back into a solid. It stays in the shape it was when it was spread.

A 250 g bar of (milk) chocolate makes 250 g of melted chocolate. The weight does not get more or less when it melts.

This experiment shows what happens to the temperature of ice as it melts to water.

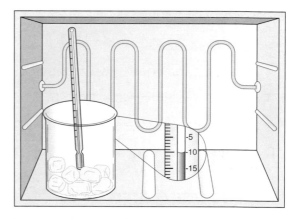

a) **Freezing** is the opposite of melting. If you touch ice in the freezer with a damp hand, your hand gets frozen onto the ice.

b) When the ice is first taken out of the freezer, it is dry and the temperature is below 0 °C.

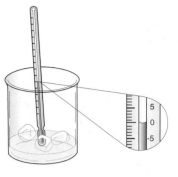

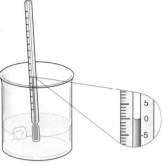

c) The ice starts to melt. When the ice is melting, the temperature is 0 °C.

d) The temperature stays at 0 °C until all the ice has melted. Even if a tiny amount of ice is left, the temperature will still be 0 °C.

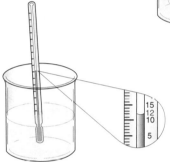

e) Only when all the ice has melted does the water in the beaker begin to get warmer.

Figure 2

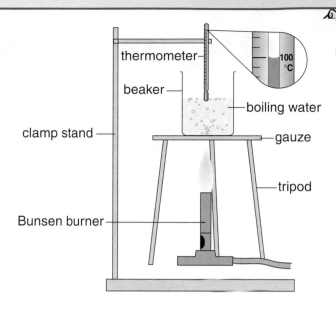

Figure 3 This is the right way to take the temperature of a boiling liquid. Don't let the thermometer touch the bottom of the beaker. Water boils at exactly 100 °C.

Questions

5 If you left the water boiling for a long time what would happen?

6 At what temperature does water boil?

Questions

1 Why does ice taste the same as water?

2 Draw three pictures of what an ice cube looks like as it melts.

3 At what temperature does ice melt?

4 At what temperature does water freeze?

Boiling

A hot chocolate drink needs hot milk. When you heat milk in a pan, it gets hotter because the hob gives it energy.

When the milk begins to boil, lots of bubbles form. The energy turns liquid milk into a gas. The gas makes the milk very frothy and it could boil over. This is because the gas takes up more room than the liquid.

Remember

Copy and complete the sentences using the words below:

energy   melting   boiling

Changing from solid to liquid is called
_____.

Changing from liquid to gas is called
_____ or evaporating. Both these changes need _____.

Gases and boiling

Key words

boiling   A liquid turning to gas because of strong heating

condensing   The gas turning back to a liquid as it cools

ethanol   A liquid fuel also called meths or alcohol

fermentation   Breaking down sugar to make ethanol

fractional distillation   Combining boiling and condensing to separate liquids

vaporise   When a liquid turns into a gas (boiling or evaporating)

Figure 2 This car runs on alcohol which is made from sugar cane.

Making a fuel

Figure 1 Sugar cane growing

In Brazil they grow lots of sugar cane. The bright tropical Sun gives the sugar cane lots of energy.

The people use some of this sugar cane to make a fuel for motor cars. The sugar is **fermented** to make a mixture of **ethanol** and water. Ethanol is a good fuel, because it burns easily. But it has to be separated from the water.

The ethanol and water mixture is heated. Ethanol boils at a lower temperature than water, so it **vaporises** first. The vapour is **condensed** to give a fuel that is nearly pure ethanol. This is called **fractional distillation**.

Questions

1   What is the fuel made from sugar called?

2   What mixture needs to be separated?

3   How do they get the fuel out of the mixture?

Boiling

Figure 3 Remember the carnival people ideas from Chapter 2?

For a liquid to turn into a gas, the particles need to move faster. They need to be moving fast enough to escape from the surface of the liquid. Heat energy makes the particles move faster.

You can see the steam rising from hot water as a few water particles escape. As the water heats up, all the particles are moving fast enough. Large 'holes' appear in the liquid and the water boils.

In a mixture of liquids, the lighter the particle, the easier it is to make it speed up. So lightweight liquid particles boil at lower temperatures. Heavier particles have a higher **boiling** point. Ethanol must have lighter particles than water, because ethanol boils at a lower temperature.

Figure 4 Raise the pressure and water boils at a higher temperature. In a pressure cooker water boils at 115°C.

Figure 5 Lower the pressure and water boils at a lower temperature. High up a mountain water boils at 80°C, so you can't make good tea.

Remember

Copy and complete the sentences using these words:

liquid   distillation   moving   boiling

B_____ happens when liquid particles are **m**_____ fast enough to escape.

Lighter particles in a **l**_____ mixture boil at a lower temperature.

You can separate liquids by fractional **d**_____.

Questions

4 What is the difference between a liquid and a gas? Draw particle pictures to explain.

5 What happens to the speed of movement of particles as they get hotter?

CHAPTER 5

Finishing off!

Remember

It's hard to tell by looking at it if a liquid is a **solution**. The dissolved material has disappeared. The mixture is **transparent** (see-through). The solution may be coloured, but so are some liquids on their own. We use lots of liquids and we don't know if they are solutions. You can separate a solution into its parts by evaporating the **solvent** and leaving the **solute** behind.

Varnish is plastic particles dissolved in white spirit.
Nail polish has shiny plastic particles dissolved in a liquid called propanone.
Food colouring has dye particles dissolved in water.
Fizzy drink has flavour and gas particles dissolved in water.

Questions

1   Take a new page in your exercise book. Make a list of all the Key Words from the boxes in this chapter down the side. Take two lines per word. Try to write the meaning of each word without looking. Then go back and fill in any you did not know or got wrong.

2   Copy and complete this table:

Solution	Solvent	Solute
varnish	white spirit	
nail polish		propanone
food colouring	water	
	water	flavour and gas

3   Where does a solvent go when the solution dries out?

4   Draw a particle picture showing a fizzy drink solution.

Web sites to visit:

Solubility Rules
http://www.chem.www.geocities.com/~jortego/chemtopics/solubility.html

Water Purification by Solar Distillation
http://www.solardome.com/SolarDome84.html

CHAPTER 6

Force and motion

Starter Activity
Diving forces

The diver stands on the diving board. There are two forces acting on her. The force of **gravity** pulls her down. The diving board pushes up on her feet. She does not move up or down so we say the forces on her are balanced.

The diver steps off the diving board. Now there is no upward force. The force of gravity pulls her down to the water.

Soon the diver hits the water. The water provides a force of **resistance** that slows the diver to a stop.

The **Earth** pulls the diver towards it. There is a force of **attraction**.

Questions

Copy and complete these sentences. Use the words in **bold**.

1 The diver is pulled down towards the **E____** by the force of **g_____**. The water provides a force of **r_____**.

   The Earth pulls things towards it. This is called a force of **a_____**.

2 Gravity is pulling you downwards. What is holding you up?

3 What is the effect of the water on the diver?

69

Speed, time and distance

Figure 1 The speedo of the car tells the driver the speed, instant by instant.

This 'speedo' shows that the car is going at 50 kilometres per hour (this is about 30 miles per hour). If the car travels at this **speed** for an hour it will travel a distance of 50 kilometres.

The quantities involved are:

speed = 50 kilometres per hour (km/h)
distance = 50 kilometres (km)
time = 1 hour (h)

These quantities are linked together by this sum.

Speed = Distance travelled / Time taken

Figure 2 The police have to protect people from speeding drivers. They use radar guns to measure the speed of cars.

Speed (km/h)	Time (h)	Distance travelled (km)
40	1	40
50	1	50
120	1	120
40	2	80
50	2	100
120	2	240

Table 1 This table shows how far the car travels in 1 hour at different speeds. It also shows how far it will travel in 2 hours.

Questions

1 Name a unit of speed.

2 A car travels at a steady speed of 60 kilometres per hour.
   a) How far does it go in 1 hour?
   b) How far will it go in 2 hours?

Figure 3 An Olympic sprinter

The sprinter runs the 100 metre race in 10 seconds. We can work out his speed.

distance = 100 metres
time = 10 seconds
speed = ?

Speed = Distance travelled / Time taken

that's 100 metres ÷ 10 seconds
100 divided by 10 is 10
So the sprinter runs at 10 metres per second
Speed = 10 metres per second.

Figure 4 A cheetah

This cheetah travels 100 metres in 4 seconds:
distance = 100 metres
time = 4 seconds
speed = ?

To find the speed we divide distance by the time.

Speed = Distance travelled / Time taken

that's 100 metres ÷ 4 seconds
100 divided by 4 is 25
So the cheetah runs at 25 metres per second
Speed = 25 metres per second.

Questions

3 **a)** A runner goes at a steady speed of 6 metres per second for 1 second. How far does she go?
b) How far will she go in: i) 2 seconds, ii) 10 seconds, iii) 100 seconds?

4 A car travels 80 kilometres in 2 hours. What is its speed?

Remember

Copy and complete the sentences. Use these words:

distance   hour   time   metres   kilometres   seconds

A speed limit in a town might be 50 **k**_____ per hour. On a motorway the speed limit might be 120 kilometres per **h**___. Sometimes it is better to measure speed in metres per second. Then distance is measured in **m**_____ and time is measured in **s**_____.
To work out speed we can write
speed = **d**_____ ÷ **t**___.

Different kinds of force

Key words

extension   The increase in length of something that has been stretched

forcemeter   An instrument to measure force

gravity   A force that attracts

magnetic force   The force caused by a magnet

newton   The unit of force

weight   The force of gravity acting on your body

On this page we find that there are different kinds of force. We can measure a force by seeing how much it stretches a spring.

The force of gravity

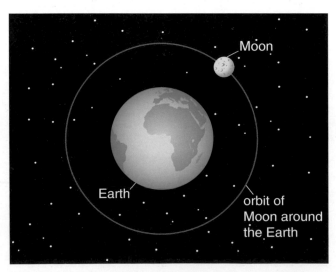

Figure 1 The force of gravity keeps the Moon in orbit around the Earth.

The force of **gravity** is a force that attracts. The Earth attracts everything towards itself. It acts above the Earth so you can still feel it when you are in an aeroplane. We all feel the force of gravity. The force of gravity acting on your body is called your **weight**.

The Moon has its own pull of gravity. The Earth and the Moon attract each other. It is this force of attraction which keeps the Moon in orbit round the Earth.

Magnetic forces

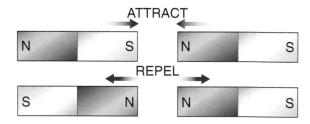

Figure 2 Forces acting between magnets.

Forces also act between two magnets. The magnets don't have to be touching each other. Magnets can push each other away. We say they 'repel' each other. They can also attract each other. The force between magnets is not a force of gravity. It is a different kind of force called a **magnetic force**.

Questions

1   Name the force which attracts things to the Earth.

2   Name the force which acts between magnets.

Stretching and measuring

A force is needed to stretch a rubber band. You can provide the force with your fingers. Or you can get gravity to provide the force by hanging masses from the rubber band.

A spring also stretches. We can use the stretch of a spring to measure force. The amount of stretch is called the **extension** of the spring. We need a spring with a hook and a scale with numbers on it for the measurements. It is called a **forcemeter**. The unit used for measuring force is called a **newton**. One newton is about the size of force needed to hold an apple.

This unit is named after Sir Isaac Newton. He was the first person to say important things about gravity and other forces. There is an old story that he saw an apple fall from a tree. This made him start to think about gravity.

Figure 3 We measure force in units called newtons. The bigger the force, the more the spring stretches.

Remember

Copy and complete the sentences. Use these words:

**newton   extension   gravity
forcemeter   repel   weight**

Magnets can attract or **r**_____ each other. The force of **g**_____ acts between big objects like the Earth and the Moon. It also acts on objects like apples. The force of gravity acting on an apple is called its **w**_____. We can measure force by measuring the **e**_____ of a spring. The unit we use for measuring force is called a **n**_____. We measure it with a **f**_____.

Questions

3   Copy and complete this table by writing 'yes' or 'no' in the spaces:

	Force of gravity	Magnetic force
Can act without touching		
Only provides forces of attraction		
Provides forces of attraction and repulsion (repelling)		

Balanced and unbalanced forces

Key words

accelerate   Go faster and faster

driving force   A force that moves you forwards

resistance force   A force that tries to stop you moving

Balanced forces can keep you going at a steady speed. Unbalanced forces can make you change speed or change direction.

Starting off

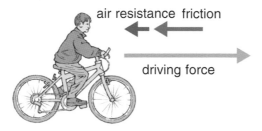

air resistance friction

driving force

Figure 1

The forward force is the **driving force** you put on the pedals. When you start off the main **resistance force** comes from the friction in the moving parts of the bike. At low speeds there is small resistance force from the air. Your driving force is bigger than the resistance forces. You go faster and faster. You **accelerate**.

Cruising along at speed

air resistance friction

driving force

Figure 2

There is more air resistance at high speed. Your driving force matches the two resistance forces. You keep going at a steady speed. You don't accelerate any more. The forces are balanced.

Stopping pedalling – slowing down gently

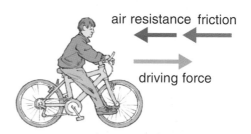

air resistance friction

driving force

Figure 3

If the driving force is very small, there is nothing to balance the friction and air resistance forces any more. The forces acting against your movement are bigger than the driving force. The forces are unbalanced. You slow down.

Braking

air resistance friction

Figure 4

If you need to stop in a hurry, you put your brakes on. This increases the friction force and you slow down quickly.

1 a) On a bike, what happens to your speed when the forces on it are balanced?

b) What happens when the driving force is bigger than the resistance forces?

c) What happens when the resistance forces are bigger than the driving force?

He's fallen for her!

Let's look at the forces on our hero as he jumps from an aeroplane at 5000 metres.

a) Our hero jumps. His weight, the gravity force, is much greater than air resistance. The forces are unbalanced. He accelerates towards the ground.

b) He falls at 200 kilometres per hour. The air resistance force has increased. It just balances the gravity force. He travels at a steady speed.

c) With the parachute open, the resistance force is much larger than the gravity force. He slows down rapidly.

d) On the ground his weight force downwards is balanced by an upwards force from the ground.

Figure 5

2 Do a simple drawing of a cyclist who is starting off and accelerating. Add arrows to show:

a) force of friction,

b) force of air resistance,

c) driving force.

3 a) Sort these situations into 'balanced force' and 'unbalanced force'

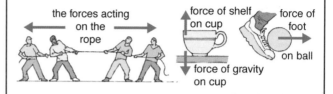

the forces acting on the rope

force of shelf on cup

force of foot on ball

force of gravity on cup

b) Which of the objects are changing speed?

Copy and complete the sentences. Use these words:

air   balanced   friction   accelerate   unbalanced   driving

When you push on the pedals of a bike you exert a **d_____** force which moves you forward. When you are moving, two forces act against your movement. They are **f_____** and **a__** resistance. When the forces are **b_____** you will keep going at a steady speed. When the forces are **u_____** your speed will change. If the driving force is bigger than the resistance forces you will **a_____**.

6.4 Wheelchair speed

Key words

air resistance (drag) A friction force when something moves through the air

friction The force that opposes movement

When objects move, there are forces which resist their movement. If we want to keep going at a steady speed there must be another force to balance the forces that resist. We call it the driving force.

Average speed

Figure 1 This is Heinz. He is a parathlete. He has just covered 42 kilometres in 2 hours.

We can work out Heinz's average speed. We say average speed because he will have gone faster and slower in different parts of the race.

Heinz's speed = $\dfrac{\text{Distance travelled}}{\text{Time taken}}$

That is 42 kilometres divided by 2 hours

Heinz's speed = 42 kilometres ÷ 2 hours

42 divided by 2 is 21

So his average speed was 21 kilometres per hour.

Wheelchair forces

Heinz has to work hard to keep up a steady speed. He has to push all the time. If he did not push, he would soon stop. There are two forces which always act against his movement. They are **air resistance** and **friction** forces.

Air resistance

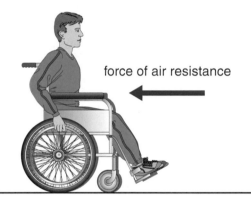

force of air resistance

Figure 2 The faster you go through the air, the more air resistance you can feel. Air resistance forces are sometimes called **drag** forces. Drag has a slowing down effect.

Friction

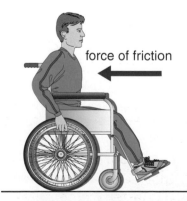

force of friction

Figure 3 It can be hard for two surfaces to slide over each other. The wheel has to slide round the axle that's holding it. Friction forces stop things sliding over each other. They have slowing down effects.

Driving force

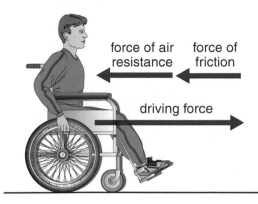

force of air resistance ← force of friction ←

driving force →

Figure 4 Heinz has to push to overcome the friction and air resistance forces which slow him down. His force is called the driving force. To keep going at a steady speed his driving force must match the friction and drag forces.

Wind resistance increases with speed

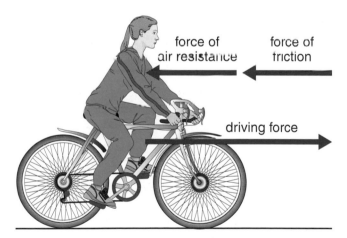

force of air resistance ← force of friction ←

driving force →

Figure 5

The cyclist has to provide a driving force to go at a steady speed. Forces of air resistance and friction act against her motion. She can feel the force of air resistance. It feels like a wind blowing in her face. The faster she goes, the bigger the air resistance.

Questions

1 A car travels 65 kilometres in 1 hour. What is its average speed?

2 Name two forces that resist movement.

3 Heinz moves his wheelchair at a steady speed. What can you say about the driving force and the resistance forces?

4 What happens to the air resistance force as you go faster?

5 A runner in a marathon race covers 42 kilometres in 3 hours.

Copy and complete:

Runner's speed = **d**_____ travelled ÷ time taken

that's 42 kilometres divided by ___ hours

Runner's speed = ___ kilometres ÷ ____ hours

____ divided by 3 is 14

The runner's average speed is ____ kilometres per hour.

Remember

Copy and complete the sentences. Use these words:

**friction   drag   resistance
              driving   time**

You can work out speed by dividing distance by **t**___. A moving object has to overcome forces of **f**_____ and air **r**_____. To move at a steady speed, the **d**_____ force must balance the resistance forces. The force of air resistance is sometimes called a **d**___ force.

Floating and swimming in water

Key words

drag Friction when moving through air or a liquid

thrust A forward push force

upthrust An upwards force exerted by water

When an object floats in water, the downward force of gravity is balanced by an upwards force from the water. Water exerts stronger **drag** forces than air does.

Figure 1 A seal floating in the sea.

A fully grown seal is a large animal. It has a lot of weight.

Diving in

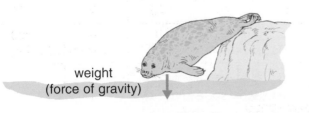

Figure 2 The seal dives off a rock. Its weight is a downwards force. It accelerates downwards because there is no upwards force to balance it.

Resting on the beach

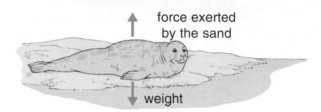

force exerted by the sand

weight

Figure 3 The seal rests on a sandy beach. The sand exerts an upwards force to balance its weight force.

Floating in the water

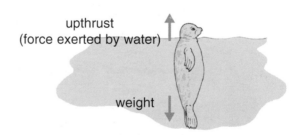

upthrust (force exerted by water)

weight

Figure 4 The seal floats in the water. The water provides an upwards force to balance its weight. This force is called an **upthrust**.

Upthrust in water

All objects in water experience an upthrust. When upthrust balances weight, the motion of the object does not change. The object floats like the seal.

Sinking

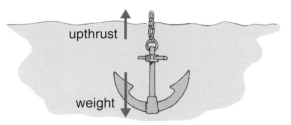

Figure 5 The anchor of a boat is made of iron. The upthrust from the water is smaller than its weight. The anchor accelerates downwards.

Dolphins on the move

Figure 6 Dolphins speed through the water.

Dolphins can swim at speeds of up to 20 metres per second.

Figure 7

A dolphin uses its flippers and strong tail to push water backwards. This backwards push on the water pushes the dolphin forwards. The forward push force is called **thrust**.

Water exerts big drag forces. Drag is a resistance force. Dolphins need strong muscles to give them enough thrust to move through the water at speed.

Remember

Copy and complete the sentences. Use these words:

thrust   drag   upthrust

An upwards force in water is called **u_____**.
A swimming dolphin experiences a resistance force called **d____**. It uses its flippers and tail to give it a forwards force called **t_____**.

Questions

1 Copy and complete the dolphin speed table.

Speed in metres per second	20	20	20	20	20	20	20
Time in seconds	1	2	3	4	10	60 (1 min)	300 (3 mins)
Distance in metres	20	40		80		1200	

2 Is the dolphin accelerating or travelling at a steady speed?

3 How far will the dolphin travel in 5 seconds?

Finishing off!

Remember

★ We can calculate the **speed** of an object if we know the **distance** it moves and the time it takes. We use the sum:

speed = distance travelled / time

★ Distance moved is usually measured in **metres** or **kilometres**.

★ Time taken is usually measured in **seconds** or **hours**.

★ Speed is usually measured in **metres per second** or **kilometres per hour**.

★ **Unbalanced forces** change the speed or direction of objects.

★ **Balanced forces** produce no change in movement.

★ **Air resistance** (or drag) and **friction** provide forces that resist movement.

★ **Upthrust** is an upwards force provided by water and other liquids.

★ We measure force in units called **newtons**.

Questions

1 Take a new page in your exercise book. Make a list of all the Key Words from the boxes in this chapter down the side. Take two lines per word. Try to write the meaning of each word without looking. Then go back and fill in any you did not know or got wrong.

2 Copy and complete this table of information. You do not need to fill in the boxes marked with a (–).

Moving object	Driving force	Forces resisting movement	Forces balanced or unbalanced	Speed – steady, increasing or decreasing	Typical speed in metres per second	Typical distance travelled in 1 second
bird flying at steady speed	force between wings and air	air resistance		steady	10	
apple falling from tree	gravity	air resistance	unbalanced		–	–
sports bag sliding across the floor	none (after it's released)	friction			–	–
'plane on runway	thrust provided by engines	air resistance, friction		increasing	–	–
'plane in steady flight			balanced		150	

Web sites to visit:

Forces & Motion Project
http://teams.lacoe.edu/documentation/projects/science/motion.html

Variation and classification

Biologists put plants and animals into groups. This is called **classification**. In your primary school you probably used keys to help you identify common plants and animals. Keys are very useful. The key on this page can be used to identify different dinosaurs. Can you name these dinosaurs using the key?

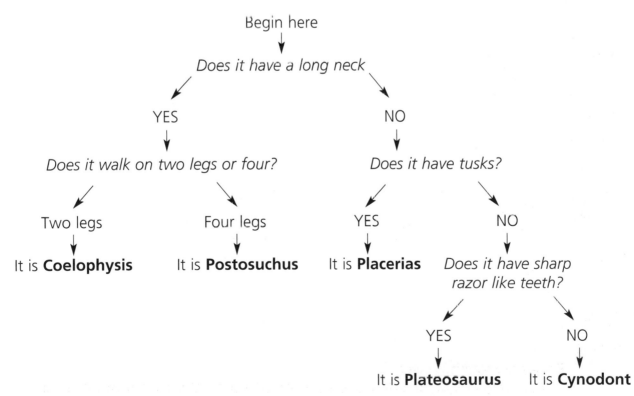

Begin here

Does it have a long neck

YES → Does it walk on two legs or four?

Two legs → It is **Coelophysis**

Four legs → It is **Postosuchus**

NO → Does it have tusks?

YES → It is **Placerias**

NO → Does it have sharp razor like teeth?

YES → It is **Plateosaurus**

NO → It is **Cynodont**

Variation

Look at the people sitting near to you. Do they look the same as you or are they different from you? They will each have lots of things that are the same: two eyes, two ears, two arms and two legs. When scientists look at the differences between living things, they are looking at what they call **variation**. Some differences or variations are easy to see.

Figure 1

Look at Figure 1. A mouse and an elephant both have four legs. But the legs are very different in shape and it is easy to see why.

Other things will be more difficult to see. Your blood group may be the same as the person sitting next to you or it may be different. You cannot tell just by looking.

Some differences can easily be put into groups. For example people can be put into groups according to their hair colour or eye colour. Other differences are not so easy to put into groups, like a person's height.

Questions

1   Can you put your classmates into groups according to their hair colour?

2   Think of three other groups you could make.

3   Which of the following would be easy to put into separate groups and which would not?
    finger length   eye colour
    foot length   arm length

Reasons for variation

Where we live and how we are brought up can cause variation, even between identical twins. If one twin eats more than the other and happens to live in a hot country, he would end up bigger and heavier than his twin. He may also have a darker skin colour from sunbathing. These differences or variations are called **environmental variation**.

If you look at your natural parents or look at the photograph in Figure 3 you will see that there are some features that run in families. These can be the shape of the nose or the type and colour of hair. This means that you will look like your natural parents or brother or sister. These are characteristics that we inherit from our parents. Scientists call this **inherited variation**.

Figure 3 You can see that the members of the Corrs family look similar.

Questions

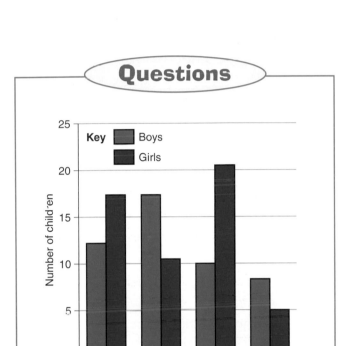

Figure 2 Hair colour in 13 year old children.

4 How many girls in the graph have auburn hair?

5 How many boys in the graph have black hair?

Remember

Copy the following paragraph and use these words to complete it:

**variations   inherited variations
hair colour
environmental variations
natural parents   weight**

When we look at the differences between people we are looking at **v**_____ between people. Some variations are passed down from our **n**_____ **p**_____, for example our **h**_____ **c**_____. We call these variations **i**_____ **v**_____. Other variations can be due to where or how we live. For example, our **w**_____ can usually be controlled by how much we eat and how healthy our diet is. These sorts of variations we call **e**_____ **v**_____.

What causes variation

People can have different features for different reasons. Sometimes where they live and how they live can alter their features. People also inherit features from their natural parents. Let's look further at inherited variation and environmental variation.

No two people are alike, unless they are identical twins. Even then there can be differences. Look at the identical twins in Figure 1. They look the same, but one of them is heavier and has a scar. Some of their features are identical, such as the shape of the nose and mouth.

Some people do not like some of the features that they inherit from their parents. They alter them by having plastic surgery.

Figure 1 Even identical twins can show differences.

Question

Make a table in your exercise book like the one below. Then do Question 1.

Features that are Inherited	Features that are environmental	Features that could be inherited or could be environmental

1   Put each of the features in the list below into your table.

hair colour

hand size

eye colour

ability to sing

being good at maths

ability to draw

ability to sing

mouth shape

skin colour

weight

height

foot size

nose shape

Figure 2 Although this dog has had its tail docked, its puppies won't be born with docked tails.

Dog breeders sometimes change how their dogs look by cutting off their tails. This is called docking. The dog in Figure 2 has had his tail docked. Changing your appearance by plastic surgery or docking the tails of dogs does not mean that the feature will be inherited. Dogs have had their tails docked for hundreds of years, but their puppies are never born without a tail.

Plants and animals can also be affected by where they grow or how they are grown. Trees in windy areas tend to be thinner.

The same type of flower grown in different types of soil may be different colours (see Figure 3).

Animals with fur that live in cold countries tend to have thicker coats than the same animal living in a warm country.

Figure 3 The colour of the hydrangea flower depends on the type of soil it grows in.

Questions

2 Give some reasons why identical twins that were separated at birth may not be identical if they met again after 30 years.

3 If a man with ears that stuck out had plastic surgery to pin them back, would it stop any of his children having the same types of ears?

Remember

Choose the correct word from each pair and copy the paragraph into your exercise book.

Features can be **inherited/lost** from your parents. Sometimes how we live or where we live can affect our features. For example, we can change the shape of our nose by having **pizza/plastic surgery**. We can also change our weight by having too much **pizza/plastic surgery**. Plants can also have their features controlled by where they are **bought/grown**. Trees planted in windy areas tend to be **fatter/thinner** than other trees of the same kind. Changing the way you look by plastic surgery will not stop that feature from being passed on to your children.

Charles Darwin

Figure 1 Charles Darwin is on the back of the £10 note.

Charles Darwin was born in England in 1809. He was the son of a doctor and came from a wealthy family.

In 1831 he sailed to South America on board a ship called *HMS Beagle*. He went on the journey to look at the **geology** (the rocks, fossils and minerals) of South America. Later on in his journey he also looked at and collected examples of plants and animals. The ship sailed around the world for five years. For Charles Darwin it was a wonderful **adventure** and the starting point of his life as a great **scientist**.

During the five years, Darwin visited many interesting places. He went to the Galapagos Islands where he found some strange animals. There were huge lizards called iguanas and giant tortoises. Darwin also collected birds from the islands. The birds looked different but were all from one family of birds – the finches. Darwin didn't realise this at the time. When he arrived back in England, the birds were **identified** and it was found that they were all **related**. What made them look different was the shape of their beaks. Scientists realised that the shape of the beak was linked to what the bird ate. Birds with big, strong beaks ate nuts. Birds with long thin beaks ate insects. They were called Darwin's finches in his honour.

Darwin was a good scientist because he noticed lots of details about the geology, plants and animals he saw on the **voyage**.

When Darwin got back to Britain he thought a lot about what he had seen. He asked questions, such as *"Why are some animals that are the same species slightly different from each other?"*.

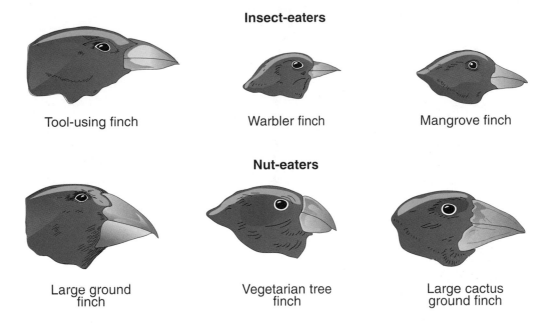

Insect-eaters

Tool-using finch

Warbler finch

Mangrove finch

Nut-eaters

Large ground
finch

Vegetarian tree
finch

Large cactus
ground finch

Figure 2 Darwin's Finches

Eventually he worked out that one kind of living thing could change slowly over a long period of time. This is called **evolution**. He also worked out that plants and animals that have features that give them an advantage over other plants and animals of the same type are more likely to survive.

A good example of this is the giraffe. Giraffes have offspring that are all slightly different. Some are taller than others. The ones with longer necks are more likely to survive than those with shorter necks because they can reach higher into the trees to eat the leaves. So they will pass on their long neck to their offspring. Darwin called this process **Natural Selection**.

Darwin wrote a famous book called *On the Origin of Species by Means of Natural Selection* to explain his ideas. It was a bestseller in 1859. Darwin died in 1882.

Questions

1   Make a list of the words in **bold** in your exercise book. Write a sentence or two about each word to explain what it means.

2   What was the name of the ship Darwin sailed on?

3   How long was the voyage?

4   Why do Darwin's finches have different types of beak?

5   Why do you think having a large beak helps a finch to eat nuts?

A select group

Selective breeding

Wheat is a very important crop. All over the world it provides food for millions of people. The wheat that we grow today is very different to the wheat grown by people thousands of years ago. Then wheat was quite a tall, thin plant with few grains. Farmers wanted to grow wheat with more grains so each plant was making more food.

They picked wheat plants with the largest number of grains and used them to pollinate other wheat plants with lots of grains. Today, the wheat that grows in the fields is much shorter and contains a larger number of grains. This is an example of **selective breeding**.

Selective breeding is not just about food production. Some people breed cats or dogs for shows. They select the cats and dogs to breed because of their features.

Plant breeders might use a plant that is **resistant** to disease to produce other plants that are resistant to disease.

Figure 1 This dog has been specially bred for herding sheep

Some plant breeders try to breed different colours of flower. Others try to breed flowers that have a certain look and smell. Rose growers often name their new species after famous people.

Figure 2 These roses were specially bred by selecting features of other roses and combining them. The rose on the left was named the Picasso rose after the famous painter. The rose on the right is called the Queen Mother rose.

Questions

1 Why might it be better to breed shorter varieties of wheat? (*Hint*: think about what could happen in different types of weather!)

2 Selective breeding could mean that some varieties of plants and animals could become extinct and die out completely. If this happens, we will lose all of their features, good and bad. Why do you think it is important to keep rare plants and animals?

Remember

Copy and complete the following passage using the words in the list below. Not all of the words are used!

**flower pollen features
characteristics varieties select
smell colour**

For many thousands of years, farmers and breeders have been breeding new **v**_____ of crops and animals. They **s**_____ plants and animals that show **f**_____ that they want and breed them with other plants and animals that have other useful features. By this method, new varieties are produced. Rose growers try to produce new varieties that have some of the features of one plant and some of the other, such as **s**_____, **c**_____ and type of **f**_____.

Belonging together

In order to make it easier for scientists to identify living organisms, they use similarities and differences between living things to place them into groups.

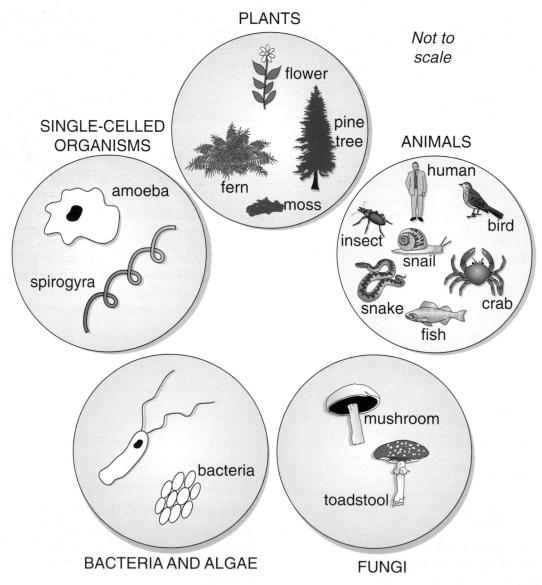

Figure 1 These are the five kingdoms that all living things can be put into.

There are so many different living things that scientists cannot tell you exactly how many different types there are. Their best guess is that there are between 2.5 and 10 million different living **species**. Scientists can put all the organisms in the world into five **kingdoms**. These are shown in Figure 1. The animal kingdom can be split again into two big groups: **vertebrates** and **invertebrates**. Vertebrates are animals with backbones like humans, cats and dogs. Invertebrates are animals without backbones, like crabs and beetles.

Scientists are finding new species of plants and animals all the time. The oceans contain lots of new species. Most of our planet is covered by water. Although 12 men have walked on the Moon, fewer than 10 people have been to the bottom of the deepest ocean. We have detailed maps of the Moon's surface, but few detailed maps of the sea floor.

Figure 2 A blue whale, the largest animal on earth.

Questions

1 Laura and Charles were talking about the differences between bats and birds. Charles said "A bird has wings and a bat has wings, therefore a bat is a bird!" Laura disagrees. What do you think? Give some reasons for your answer.

2 Put the following organisms into their correct kingdom.

bee, garden spider, rose, rabbit, amoeba, goldfish, pine tree, mushroom, earthworm, carnation

Remember

Write the names of the five kingdoms across the top of a page in your exercise book. Below each one add the names of organisms that you can think of that belong in that kingdom.

Clones

A **clone** is an exact copy of a plant or an animal. Identical twins are clones of each other. A plant that is grown from a cutting will also be a clone. Scientists have recently been able to make clones of animals in the laboratory.

Figure 1 Dolly the sheep – the first cloned mammal.

The first known clone of a mammal was Dolly the sheep. Dolly was created at the Roslyn Institute in Edinburgh. Dolly was created by taking an egg from a female sheep, taking out the nucleus of the cell and putting in a new nucleus from the cell of a fully grown sheep. The egg then developed into an exact copy of the sheep from which the nucleus was taken.

Step 1: Take a cell from the sheep you want to clone (the donor) and grow it in a Petri dish with chemicals that stop the nucleus from working.

Step 2: Take an egg cell from a female sheep and take out the nucleus.

Step 3: Join the adult cell with the empty egg cell using an electric spark. The nucleus starts working again.

Step 4: The cell begins to grow and divide.

Step 5: The cells are transferred to the mother's womb to grow and develop as normal.

Step 6: Lambs are produced that are identical to the donor sheep.

Figure 2 How Dolly was cloned.

Making clones of animals is very difficult. Making clones of plants is very easy. Gardeners make clones when they take cuttings from plants and grow new plants from them. Strawberries have runners that grow away from the main plant and produce small plants on the end of the runners. These can take root and a new plant will grow, identical to the parent plant.

Cloning: right or wrong?

Scientists have said that it is possible to produce human clones. They also believe that it will be possible to grow human organs that can then be used as 'back-up' organs for people in case their main organs are damaged or diseased. There is a big problem with human cloning though. Many of the clones would die before they grow to full size and some may suffer from health problems and die early.

Figure 3 Salma (on the left) and Jenny are discussing cloning

Questions

Look at the cartoon above. Who do you think has the best argument? If you were talking to Salma, what would you say about having human clones?

Remember

Carry on the conversation between Salma and Jenny. Create some new characters, or join the argument yourself. Try to give as many reasons as you can either for or against human clones.

Finishing off!

Remember

Variation

- Individuals in a species can vary in many ways, e.g. size, hair colour, eye colour.

- Some characteristics are **inherited**.

- Some characteristics are caused by the **environment**.

- Individuals may look like their parents but are not identical to them.

- **Selective breeding** can produce plants and animals with the best/most useful characteristics.

- **Clones** are offspring that are identical to their parent or another individual (e.g. an identical twin).

Classifying

- Biologists group plants and animals according to their similarities.

- The smallest group is called a **species**.

- The largest group forms a **kingdom**.

- There are five kingdoms: Plants, Animals, Fungi, Single-celled organisms and Bacteria/Blue-green algae.

Questions

1 Take a new page in your exercise book. Make a list of all the Key Words from the boxes in this chapter down the side. Take two lines per word. Try to write the meaning of each word without looking. Then go back and fill in any you did not know or got wrong.

2 What do scientists often use to try and help them identify different types of plants and animals?

3 What do we mean when we say that an animal is an
   a) invertebrate?
   b) vertebrate?

4 Which of the following animals are invertebrates and which are vertebrates?

   spider, dolphin, cat, snake, fly, crab, human being, frog, worm, centipede, locust, trout

5 One large group of animals that no longer exists is the dinosaurs. How do we know that they were vertebrates?

6 What are the five kingdoms that biologists use to group all living things?

Web sites to visit:

New Scientist magazine report on cloning
   http://www.newscientist.com/hottopics/cloning

Evolution of the Horse
   http://www.facethemusic.org/evolution.html

Acids, alkalis and salts

Starter Activity
A sour taste

Beware acids!

Acid is a word everybody knows. But what is an acid?

Battery acid is used in car batteries. Bottles of acid are used in school. These are dangerous acids. They will have a warning label on them.

But there are lots of safe acids. Lemons, oranges, milk, vinegar and 'sour ball' sweets all contain acids.

Acids are used a lot in cooking. They add taste to food.

You may also have heard of chemicals called **alkalis**. These are the chemical opposite of acids. But take care, for they can be just as dangerous as acids. Alkalis taste very nasty, just like soap.

Acids and alkalis react with each other. They cancel each other out and make new substances that are completely safe. These new substances are called **salts**.

Questions

1   Make a list of all the 'sour' tasting substances you can think of. These are all acids.

2   Adverts on TV talk about acid indigestion. What sort of chemicals could you use to stop indigestion?

3   Bacteria on our teeth produce acid. What does the acid do to our teeth?

4   Soap is a very weak alkali. What does it feel like if you get it in your eyes?

Chemical opposites

Key words

acid   A sour tasting substance that can be dangerous

alkali   A soapy tasting substance that can be dangerous

indicator   A chemical that changes colour in acids and alkalis

neutral   A solution that is not acid or alkali

Acids and **alkalis** are chemical opposites. Acids and alkalis are two different families of chemical substances. Families of chemicals have similar reactions.

Figure 1 Beverley testing for acids and alkalis.

All acids will change the colour of some chemicals. These coloured chemicals are called **indicators**. Litmus is a type of indicator. When litmus is dissolved in pure water (neutral) it is purple. Acids change litmus to a red colour and alkalis make litmus blue. **Neutral** substances do not change the colour of litmus.

Beverley wanted to find out if any of the things in her kitchen contained acids. She got lots of substances from the kitchen and tested them with litmus paper.

Substance tested	Colour with red litmus paper	Colour with blue litmus paper
lemon juice	did not change	red
salt	did not change	did not change
soap	blue	did not change
cola drink	did not change	red
baking soda	blue	did not change
bottled water	did not change	did not change
tomato sauce	did not change	red
yoghurt	did not change	red

Questions

1   Make a list of the substances that turn blue litmus to red.

2   Put a tick if these substances keep red litmus red.

3   Put the heading 'acids' at the top of this list.

4   Make a list of the substances that turn red litmus to blue.

5   Put a heading 'alkalis' at the top of this list.

6   Make a list of the two substances left. Put 'neutral' as your heading.

Using acids

Lots of things we use everyday contain acids:

- metal cleaner: acid particles make the dull surface on metals wash off easily.

- vitamin C: this is added to food so it will not go bad.

- aspirin: there are acids in aspirin.

Thinking about acids

Figure 2 Acid particles behave like these nippy mice.

Acid particles are a bit like mice. They are little nippy particles that move about 'biting' other particles and making them change.

Using alkalis

Figure 3 These things all contain alkalis.

Alkalis have different particles in them. Alkalis are often used to dissolve grease. Soap is an alkali. Oven cleaner is a very strong alkali.

Alkali particles do not taste nice at all. That's why toothpaste and indigestion tablets always have a strong flavour added.

Remember

Copy and complete the sentences using these words:

**red   opposite   litmus   indicators
acids   substances**

Acids are a family of **s**_____.

This means that all **a**____ will do the same chemical changes. All acids turn litmus **r**___.

Alkalis are the **o**_____ of acids. Alkalis turn **l**____ blue. Chemicals like litmus are called **i**_____.

Measuring acids

Key words

concentrated Lots of particles in the solution

pH scale Scale of numbers used to measure acidity

Universal Indicator Special indicator with lots of colour changes. It can be paper or solution

Acids and alkalis are not all the same strength. The most dangerous are concentrated solutions.

Universal Indicator

Universal Indicator can go different colours. It changes to show how **concentrated** the acid or alkali in a solution is.

The pH scale

There is a special scale for measuring acidity. It is called the **pH scale**.

You can get the pH scale number by using the colour of Universal Indicator and matching it.

Less dangerous acids	More dangerous acids
citric acid – lemonade tartaric acid – baking powder ethanoic acid – vinegar	sulphuric acid – car batteries nitric acid – cleaning metals hydrochloric acid – weak solution in the stomach

Table 1 Some acids are more dangerous than others.

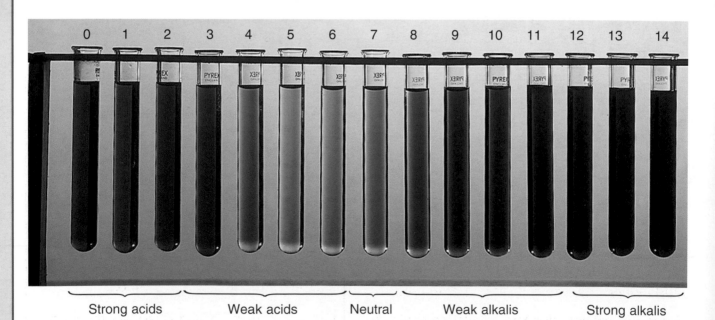

Figure 1 The colour range of Universal Indicator. The numbers above the tubes are the pH number.

Questions

Copy and complete this table.

Solution	pH scale number	Colour of Universal Indicator paper
1 black coffee	5	
2 lime water	12	
3 blood	8	
4 sea water		green
5 milk		yellow
6 ammonia solution (surface cleaner)	11	
7 oven cleaner (sodium hydroxide)		purple
8 rust remover (phosphoric acid)		red

Why are acids dangerous?

Figure 2 The savage acid particle (H) and the savage alkali particle (OH).

Acids can be dangerous because they are like little savage particles. These particles are only made when the acid is dissolved in water.

When it dissolves, the acid substance splits up into smaller particles. There will be the savage particles and other particles as well.

The savage acid particles react with metals and rocks to dissolve them. They will also destroy your skin and hurt like a burn.
If there are only a few acid particles, your tough leathery skin can cope. They will even tickle your taste buds (like in lemonade).

Alkali substances also dissolve to produce harmful particles. They are just as savage as acids. They will attack grease in your skin and even wood.

Remember

Copy and complete the sentences using these words:

concentrated   indicator   scale   strong

The pH **s**_____ is used to measure how **s**_____ an acid or alkali is.

Universal **I**_____ goes different colours in different strengths of acid solution.

C_____ acids and alkalis are the most dangerous.

Salt and water

Acids and alkalis come together to make new substances. The savage particles join to make ordinary water particles. This is called **neutralisation**. What is left of the acid and the alkali makes a substance called a salt.

acid + alkali → salt + water

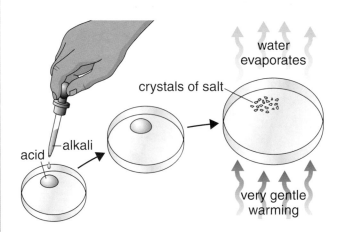

Figure 1 Place two or three drops of acid on a petri dish. Add the same amount of alkali. Mix with the end of the dropper and heat very gently. The water evaporates leaving crystals of salt.

Making salts

To show when the solution is exactly neutral you need an indicator.

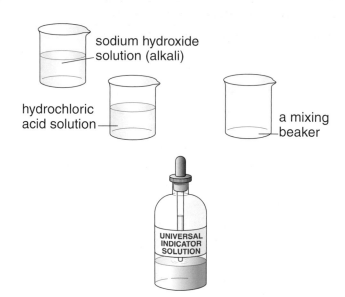

a) Equipment for making a neutral solution.

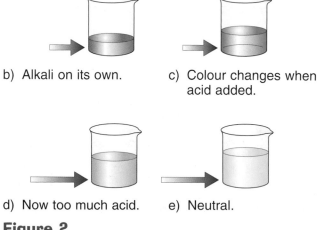

b) Alkali on its own.

c) Colour changes when acid added.

d) Now too much acid.

e) Neutral.

Figure 2

When you have made the solution exactly neutral, you will have the salt you want with no acid or alkali particles left. If you leave the solution, the water will evaporate leaving crystals of salt.

Naming the salt

You can work out the name of the salt from the names of the acid and alkali that made it.

First part of name from alkali		Second part of name from acid
sodium hydroxide makes 'sodium'	with	hydrochloric acid makes 'chloride'
potassium hydroxide makes 'potassium'	with	sulphuric acid makes 'sulphate'
calcium hydroxide makes 'calcium'	with	nitric acid makes 'nitrate'
magnesium hydroxide makes 'magnesium'	with	ethanoic acid makes 'ethanoate'

Table 1 Naming salts

Questions

1 What two new substances are made when acids and alkalis neutralise each other?

2 Name the salts that are made from:
   a) potassium hydroxide and sulphuric acid
   b) calcium hydroxide and hydrochloric acid
   c) magnesium hydroxide and ethanoic acid (vinegar)

Questions

3 Is Milk of Magnesia an acid or an alkali?

4 Why does it cure heartburn?

5 Stomach acid is hydrochloric acid. Milk of Magnesia contains magnesium hydroxide. What type of salt is made when the Milk of Magnesia cures heartburn?

The stomach acid problem

Figure 3 Lucy's Dad has painful heartburn.

Lucy's dad has a problem. His stomach produces too much acid. This rises up and hurts his food tube. This is called **heartburn**.

Lucy goes to the pharmacist and gets Milk of Magnesia. Milk of Magnesia has a pH of 9. Lucy's dad swallows the medicine and after 5 minutes he feels better.

Remember

Copy and complete the sentences using these words:

salt   neutralisation   water   alkali particles

Acid **p_____** and **a_____** particles come together to make **w____**.

The other bits left behind combine to make a **s____**.

This process is called **n_____**.

Safety with acids

Key words

corrosive Damages flesh
flammable Can catch fire
goggles Made to protect the eyes
toxic Poisonous

Hazard symbols

Many chemicals are dangerous. They are marked with symbols that tell you how they can harm you.

Oxidising
These substances provide oxygen which allows other materials to burn more fiercely.

Highly flammable
These substances easily catch fire.

Toxic
These substances can cause death. They may have their effects when swallowed or breathed in or absorbed through the skin.

Harmful
These substances are similar to toxic substances but less dangerous.

Corrosive
These substances attack and destroy living tissues, including eyes and skin.

Irritant
These substances are not corrosive but can cause reddening ot blistering of the skin.

Figure 1 The common hazard symbols

Concentrated acids

These are very dangerous. Concentrated hydrochloric acid and concentrated nitric acid give off fumes. It is safe to use very small quantities in the laboratory. Usually you would only use concentrated acids inside a fume cupboard.

Hot spot

Concentrated sulphuric acid is a heavy, oily liquid. If you dilute it you must be careful. When you mix it with water it transfers energy as heat. This makes the liquids get very hot and boil.

The rule is to ADD ACID TO WATER. Then only a small amount of heat is released. NEVER add water to the concentrated acid.

Figure 2 This is what concentrated acid does to cloth. Think what it could do to your skin!

1 Which do you think is worse: 'toxic' or 'harmful'? Explain why.

2 What is the difference between 'corrosive' and 'irritant'?

3 Why are the hazard labels bright orange?

4 "A lab coat is no protection against an acid spill." Explain why this is true.

★ Safety glasses prevent acid from getting into the eyes.

   Goggles are even better because they fit close to the face and no liquid can dribble through.

★ Strong rubber gloves and rubber aprons are used by people who work a lot with strong acids.

★ Ordinary plastic gloves are often used when pouring out acids. The dribbles from the neck of the bottle can get on to the outside.

★ Eye-wash bottles are kept where acids are used.

Staying safe

There are three important rules for working with chemicals:

1 **Protect your eyes AT ALL TIMES**
   It may not be your accident. Your eyes are the most easily damaged part of your body.

2 **Never lift chemicals above eye level**
   And don't crouch down near benches.

3 **Treat any spills on the skin or eyes with lots of cold water**
   Do it immediately, but don't run, as this could cause more accidents.

Questions

5 Which part of your body is most easily damaged by chemicals?

6 Write a set of instructions for using an eye-wash bottle. Then check to see if you missed anything out.

Safety equipment

Figure 3 Safety equipment being used in the lab.

Remember

Draw the hazard labels and test yourself until you know them.
Draw cartoons to illustrate the three safety rules for chemicals to someone who does not understand English very well.

IMPORTANT: Strong alkalis are just as dangerous as acids.

Finishing off!

Acids are very useful chemical particles. They are a family of similar substances.

Acids have lots of properties that are the same.

All acids:

★ taste sour.

★ neutralise alkali solutions.

★ produce salts when they are neutralised.

★ turn litmus red.

★ turn Universal Indicator red.

★ give a pH number of less than 7 (pH 7 is a neutral solution).

Figure 1 The savage acid particle (H) and the savage alkali particle (OH).

All acids dissolve to produce savage reactive particles and a non nasty bit. The other part of the acid particle just looks on while the savage bits go about their business of tearing other chemicals apart.

That's why all acid reactions are the same.

Questions

1 Take a new page in your exercise book. Make a list of all the Key Words from the boxes in this chapter down the side. Take two lines per word. Try to write the meaning of each word without looking. Then go back and fill in any you did not know or got wrong.

2 Name the salts made when these chemicals are mixed:

a) Calcium hydroxide and hydrochloric acid

b) Sodium hydroxide and sulphuric acid

3 Draw a picture showing the colours that Universal Indicator goes in different strengths of acid and alkali.

4 Make a safety poster about hazardous substances.

Web sites to visit:

Acids, Bases, Buffers
http://www.dist214.k12.il.us/users/asanders/acid.html

pH Tutorial Launch Pad
http://www.science.ubc.ca/~chem/tutorials/pH/launch.html

The pH factor
http://www.miamisci.org/ph/ph0.html

Electric circuits

Look at John's drawing. It shows an electric circuit which has:

- a **battery** to supply energy to the circuit

- a **lamp** which will light when electricity flows through it

- a **switch** to turn the lamp on and off

- **connecting wire** to join everything together in a complete loop.

Things like lamps, motors and buzzers are called **components**.

John uses simple picture symbols to make the circuit easy to draw.

Questions

1 Copy the circuit diagram from the picture.
   a) Add a label to show which part lights up.
   b) Add a label to show which part supplies energy to the circuit.
   c) Add a label to show which part switches the circuit on and off.

2 Name four things at home which have motors in them.

Energy for life

circuit A number of electrical components and wires connected together

component Part of a circuit

current A flow of electricity

Lamps and heaters get warm when electricity goes through them. They transfer energy to things around them.

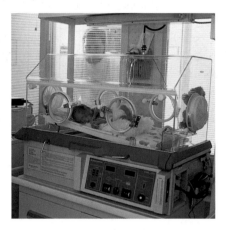

Figure 1 The heater in the incubator keeps the baby warm.

There is a heater wire in the incubator to keep the baby warm.

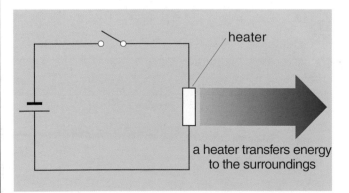

heater

a heater transfers energy to the surroundings

Figure 2 The heater circuit in the incubator has a battery, a heater wire, a switch and connecting wires.

An electric **current** in the heater wire makes it warm. The heat energy from the wire warms the incubator and keeps the baby alive. It is easy to make a heater **circuit** using the **components** in Figure 2.

Circuit symbols

When we draw an electric circuit we use symbols to make it easier to draw.

Part of circuit (component)	Symbol
Battery or cell	
Switch	
Heater or resistor	

Table 1

A heater circuit with warning lamp

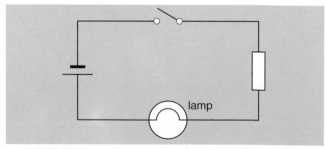

lamp

Figure 3 The heater circuit has a lamp, heater, switch, battery and connecting wires.

A real incubator circuit will have more components. This one has a lamp so that you can see if the heater is on. Let's connect up this circuit.

Figure 4 a) Look carefully at the circuit diagram.

b) Get the components. Set them out in the same order as in the circuit diagram.

c) Start at the battery. Use the connecting wire to join the components together.

d) Work your way round the circuit until you get back to the battery.

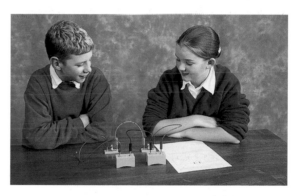

e) Switch on and it works!

Questions

1 Draw symbols for:
   a) a battery, b) a lamp and c) a switch.

2 Draw a circuit with a battery and a lamp.

Remember

Copy and complete the sentences. Use these words:

**switch   energy   symbols   lamps
heaters**

A battery transfers **e___** into a circuit. A **s___** is used to control the current in the circuit. Components are things like **l___** and **h___**. When we draw diagrams we use **s___** for the different components.

Current control

Key words

ammeter A device for measuring current
amps (A) The unit of current
series circuit A circuit with all the components in a single loop

In a river, the current is the size of the flow of water. There will be a large flow in a wet winter and a small flow in a dry summer.
An electric current is the size of the flow of electricity round the circuit.
Here are some other kinds of flow around circuits.

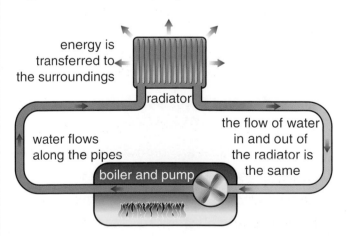

Figure 1 A flow of people around a circuit.

Figure 2 A flow of water around a central heating circuit.

An electric circuit is a bit like the flow of water in a central heating circuit.
Look to see which things are the same in Figure 2 and Figure 3.

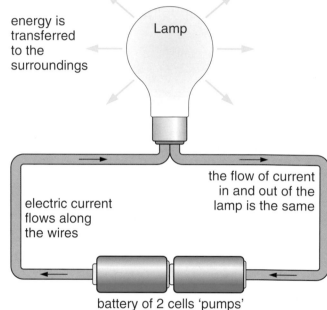

Figure 3 A flow of electric current around a circuit.

A simple circuit, like the incubator on page 106, has one loop. It is called a **series circuit**.

Measuring electric current

We use an **ammeter** to measure electric current. We measure current in **amps (A)**.

Figure 4 An ammeter reads the current in the circuit.

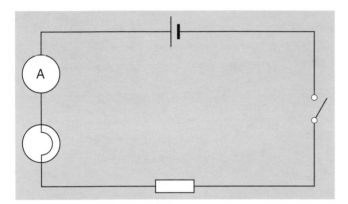

Figure 5 A circuit with an ammeter.

The ammeter goes into the circuit so that the current flows through it. The ammeter is another component in the series circuit.

Some ammeters, like the one in Figure 4, show the current as a number.

Figure 6 An ammeter scale.

The ammeter in Figure 6 has a pointer which moves along the scale. It can measure from 0 up to 1.0 amps. The reading on the ammeter is 0.4 A. A stands for amps.

Questions

What is the reading on these ammeters?

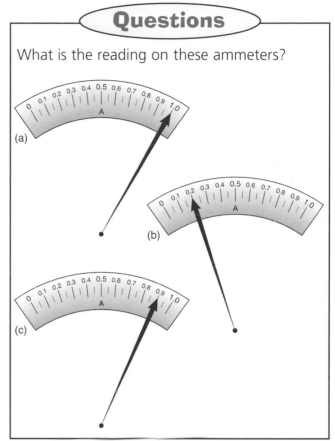

(a)

(b)

(c)

Remember

Copy and complete these sentences. Use these words:

**pump   ammeter   series   current
amps   scale**

An electric circuit with a single loop is called a **s___** circuit. A battery in an electric circuit acts like a **p___** in a central heating circuit. We use an **a___** to measure the size of the **c___** in a circuit. We take a reading from the **s___** of the ammeter. The current is measured in **a____**.

Components and currents

Figure 1 There are many circuits in an aeroplane.

Each of the circuits in Figure 1 has an ammeter measuring the current. The size of the current depends on the components in the circuit. Components resist the flow of current. We say the components have **resistance**. The more resistance they have, the more difficult it is for current to flow.

When the resistance of a component changes, the current changes. An ammeter will measure how much the current has changed.

Key words

parallel circuit A circuit which provides two or more pathways for the electric current

resistance Opposing the flow of current

Resistance of two or more components

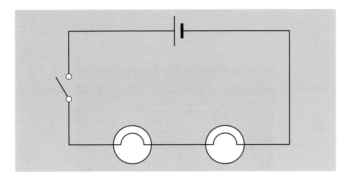

Figure 2 Lamps connected in series.

The lamps in this circuit are connected in series. Two lamps resist current *more* strongly than one. So there will be *less* current in this circuit than in a circuit with the same battery and just one lamp.

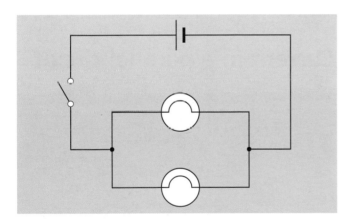

Figure 3 Lamps connected in parallel.

The lamps in this circuit are connected side by side. We say they are **in parallel**. They both have resistance, but the current has a 'choice' of two routes through the circuit. The two lamps in parallel have *less* resistance than just one lamp. There is *more* current in this circuit than in the circuit with one lamp.

Figure 4 shows a central heating circuit. Try to spot what looks like the electrical circuit in Figure 3.

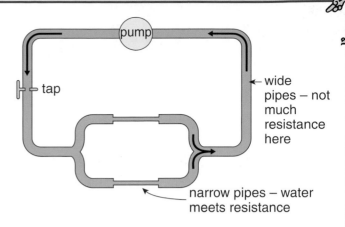

Figure 4 Water can go round and round a circuit – a bit like an electric current.

Questions

1 What happens to the current if more lamps are added in series in a circuit?

2 What happens to the current if more lamps are added in parallel with each other?

Remember

Copy and complete the sentences. Use these words:

current   circuit   resist   ammeter   parallel   bigger

The number and type of components in a **c**___ affect the current. The current can be measured with an **a**___. Most components **r**___ current. When components are added in series then the total resistance is **b**___. When components are added in **p**___ then the total resistance is smaller. The bigger the resistance, the smaller the **c**___ if the battery doesn't change.

Circuits, currents and fuses

> **Key word**
>
> **fuse** A weak point in an electric circuit. It melts when the current gets too high

Current in a series circuit

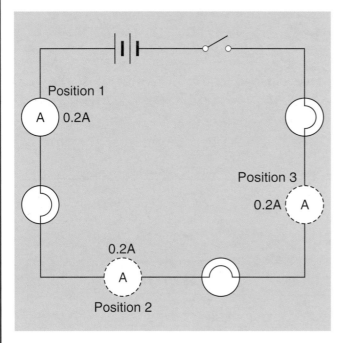

Figure 1 The ammeter shows that the current is the same at all points in a series circuit.

When the series circuit is set up, the ammeter can be placed in different positions. If the ammeter is moved to positions 2 and 3, the reading is the same. Electric current is not used up in a circuit.

If any of the lamps are unscrewed from their holders, all the lamps go out. Series circuits are not often used. Think what would happen at home if your house lights were wired in series and one lamp blew.

Figure 2 Some Christmas tree lights are wired in series.

Current in a parallel circuit

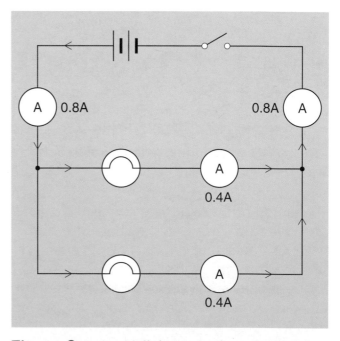

Figure 3 In a parallel circuit, the current splits and then joins up again. The current that goes back to the battery is exactly the same as the current that came from it.

The current in this parallel circuit splits two ways. The ammeters show that the current that goes back to the battery is exactly the same as the current that came from it. Current is not used up in a parallel circuit. If either lamp is unscrewed from its holder, the other one stays on. Car and house circuits are wired in parallel.

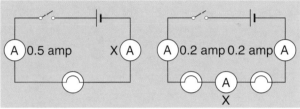

Figure 5 The circuit symbol for a fuse.

Fuses protect the wires in house and car circuits. They are very cheap to replace. It would cost a lot more to rewire your house or car.

Questions

1   Draw a circuit diagram to show three lamps in series with a switch and ammeter. What would happen if one of the lights stopped working?

2   Draw a circuit diagram to show three lamps in parallel with each other. What would happen if one of the lamps stopped working?

What if the current is too big?

When a large electric current goes through a wire, the wire gets hot.

Think of the wires in your house. A large current going through the wires might make them so hot that they melt and cause a fire. To protect the wires we use a small length of thin wire. This wire melts quickly if it gets hot and cuts off the supply of electricity. It is called a **fuse**. Quite often it is placed inside a little tube

Figure 4 The 13 amp fuse protects the wire to the electrical equipment.

Questions

3   What measurement would you expect on the ammeters marked X in each of these circuits?

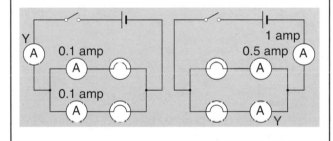

4   What measurement would you expect on the ammeters marked Y in each of these circuits? (The lamps are identical.)

Remember

Copy and complete the sentences. Use these words:

fuse   same   back   joins

The current that flows from a battery is the same as the current that flows **b___** to the battery.

When lamps are in series, each one has the **s___** current. When the lamps are in parallel the current splits and then **j___** up again. A thin wire that melts when the current gets too big is called a **f___**.

Electrical supplies

Key words

cells/battery   A chemical packet to transfer energy as electricity

voltage   The strength of an electricity supply

volts   The unit for measuring voltage

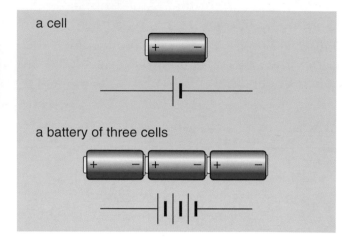

a cell

a battery of three cells

Figure 2 A single cell (top) and a battery of three cells (bottom).

Cell measurements

Every cell or battery has a measurement on it. The unit of measurement is written as V, which stands for **volts**.

Most cells have a **voltage** of 1.5 volts. A battery of two cells will have a voltage of 3 volts. The battery shown in Figure 2 has a voltage of 4.5 volts.

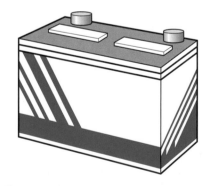

Figure 3 A 12 volt car battery has 6 cells, each cell is 2 volts.

Figure 1 Cells and batteries

The photograph shows a collection of **cells** and **batteries**. Is a cell the same as a battery? A cell transfers energy from the chemicals in it to electricity. A battery is really two or more cells joined together. A battery contains cells that are usually joined in series.

Questions

1   What is the difference between a battery and a cell?

2   Four cells are connected in series to make a battery. If each cell is 1.5 V, what is the voltage of the battery?

Cells and current

The size of the current in a circuit depends on two things:

- the number and type of components in a circuit and how they are connected

- the number and strength of the cells.

So the more cells we put in a circuit, the bigger the current that flows.

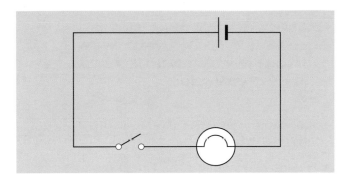

Figure 4 A torch circuit with a 3V lamp.

The lamp in this torch circuit is marked 3 V. When connected to a 1.5 V cell, the current is very weak. The lamp is very dim.

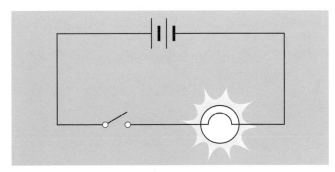

Figure 5 The 3V lamp glows brightly when connected to a 3V battery.

The 3 volt battery pushes a much larger current round the circuit and the lamp glows brightly. A 4.5 V battery would push too large a current so the lamp would burn out in minutes.

Electricity at home

The mains electricity in your home isn't driven by cells or batteries. It comes from very large generators in power stations. The supply voltage to your house is 230 volts. It is a very large voltage and it can easily produce big currents.

If you touch a wire at 230 volts then your body becomes part of the circuit. A current will flow through your body and will be large enough to kill you. This is electrocution. Mains electricity is dangerous.

When your skin is wet it has less resistance. There will be an even bigger current through your body. A big current is more dangerous. That's why you will never find any sockets in your bathroom.

Question

3 Why is it dangerous to take electrical equipment into a bathroom?

Remember

Copy and complete the sentences. Use these words:

**current   battery   dangerous
voltage   mains**

A number of cells working together is called a **b___**. The more cells in a circuit, the larger the **c___** flowing round the circuit. The 'strength' of a cell or battery is called its **v___**. Voltage is measured in units called volts. The electrical supply in our homes is called the **m___** supply. It is at a high voltage and is more **d___** than a cell or battery.

Finishing off!

Remember

★ Lamps and switches are components of **circuits**.

★ In an electric circuit with a single loop all the components are connected one after the other. They are **in series**.

★ In an electric circuit, components can be connected side by side. They are **in parallel**.

★ Circuits can transfer energy to their surroundings by heating.

★ A **cell** is a chemical package which transfers energy as electricity.

★ A **battery** is two or more cells working together.

★ We use **ammeters** to measure electric current. The unit of electric current is the **amp**.

★ The size of the current depends on the number of cells. We call the strength of a cell its **voltage**. The unit of voltage is the **volt**.

★ The size of the current in a circuit also depends on the components – how many and what kind.

★ Components of circuits have **resistance**.

★ The current leaving a battery is the same as the current returning to it. Current is not 'used up' by the components.

★ The **mains** electricity supply has a voltage of 230 V. It can make a big current flow. It is dangerous.

★ When your skin is wet it has a low resistance. A larger current can flow through your body when your skin is wet. This is very dangerous.

★ When a current flows through your body it can stop your heart working. This is **electrocution**.

★ **Fuses** can switch off a circuit by melting. They do this when the current is too big for them.

Questions

1 Take a new page in your exercise book. Make a list of all the Key Words from the boxes in this chapter down the side. Take two lines per word. Try to write the meaning of each word without looking. Then go back and fill in any you did not know or got wrong.

2 Make a poster of a house. Show where you will find components and switches. Show what supplies the electricity. Part of your poster should deal with safety issues.

Web sites to visit:

DC Circuits
http://www.physics.uoguelph.ca/tutorials/ohm/index.html

Science with Electrical Circuits
http://www.cpo.com/CPOCatalog./EC/ec_sci.htm

CHAPTER 10

Habitats, adaptation and chains

Starter Activity
A place to live

In this chapter you will learn about the places that plants and animals live – their **habitats** – and how they are adapted to living there. We will also look at food chains and webs, what eats what and how they are linked together.

We live in what is called a **temperate** region (this is something you might have learned about in geography). This means that the weather is neither tropical – hot and humid – nor polar – cold and icy. It's in between!

Questions

1 What plants and animals can you name from each of the habitats below?

2 Choose one animal from each habitat and explain how it has adapted to its habitat?

3 Try and write out one food chain for one of the habitats. Remember to include a plant at the start, an animal that eats plants and an animal that eats other animals.

Is there life on Mars?

Life on Mars

Living organisms are found in many different places on Earth. Can life exist on any of the other planets in our Solar System? Some scientists believe that life did exist on Mars billions of years ago.

Questions

1 Read the following description of a Martian from H.G. Wells' story *War of the Worlds*:

"They were huge, round bodies, or rather heads, about four feet in diameter; each body had in front of it a face. This face had no nostrils – indeed the Martians do not seem to have had any sense of smell – but it had a pair of very large, dark coloured eyes, and just beneath this a kind of fleshy beak. In a group around the mouth were 16 slender, almost whiplike tentacles arranged in two bunches of eight each."

Try to draw a picture of Wells' Martian. Could this Martian really live on Earth?

Figure 1 View of Mars – the red planet – from space. You can see the white polar cap at the top. This is a mixture of ice and dust.

What is the evidence for life on Mars

Figure 2 The surface of Mars is dry and rocky.

Figure 3 The meteorite ALH 84001.

In 1984 a potato-sized lump of rock was found in Antarctica (see Figure 3). It turned out to be a **meteorite** that had fallen to Earth 13 000 years ago. Nobody took much notice of the rock until they found that gas trapped in tiny bubbles in the rock was identical to the gases found in the thin atmosphere of Mars.

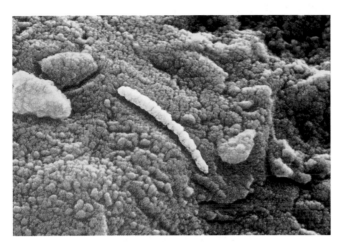

Figure 4 The first signs of alien life?

When the scientists looked at the Mars rock they found what looked like tiny **fossilised** bacteria (see Figure 4). These could be the first signs of alien life! Not all scientists agree with this. But they do agree that millions of years ago Mars had more of an atmosphere than it has today and that water ran over its surface. If you look at the photo of the surface of Mars (see Figure 5) you can see channels which water ran through.

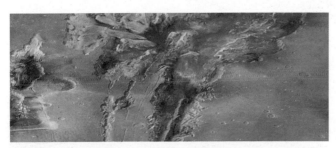

Figure 5 These channels on the surface of Mars were formed by running water.

	Mars	Earth
diameter	6766 km	12,756 km
length of day	24.62 hours	24 hours
length of year	687 days	365.25 days
average temperature	−63 °C	15 °C

Atmosphere	Mars	Earth
nitrogen	2.7%	78%
oxygen	0.13%	21%
carbon dioxide	95.32%	0.04%
other gases	1.85%	0.96%

Table 1 Comparing Mars and Earth.

What do you think it would be like living on Mars? Look at Table 1 above and try to answer the following questions. Remember to give reasons for your answers.

2 Would it be hotter or colder on average than on Earth?

3 Would the days be longer or shorter than Earth's days?

4 Would a Mars year be longer or shorter than an Earth year?

5 Would there be enough oxygen for people to breathe?

Remember

Use these words to copy and complete the sentences below:

Solar System   little   carbon dioxide

Life may have existed on other planets in the S_____ S_____. Mars has an atmosphere but it contains lots of c_____ d_____ gas, and l_____ oxygen.

Jungles, deserts and ice palaces

Key words

ecologist The name given to scientists who study where plants and animals live

habitat The place where plants and animals live

Where are living things found?

Living things have been found in all types of places around the world, from deep in the ice at Antarctica to the bottom of the oceans. We call these places **habitats**. Living things adapt to the conditions they find themselves in.

What lives where?

Think about the animals in Figure 1 for a moment. Each of these animals is in the wrong habitat. The penguin is in the jungle, the scorpion is on the ice of Antarctica and the gorilla is in the desert.

Figure 1 These animals are all in the wrong place!

A heathland

Even in Britain we have different habitats that contain different types of plants and animals that have adapted to where they live. Some of these habitats are shown in Figure 2.

What is an ecologist?

An **ecologist** is a scientist who studies where plants and animals live. Ecologists do surveys and list the different types of plants and animals they find. They also study what happens to habitats when they are damaged by human activity or pollution.

A rocky sea shore

Questions

1 What problems would each of the animals in Figure 1 have living in these places?

2 How would they have to adapt in order to survive?

3 List two places on Earth where humans cannot survive without special clothes and equipment to help us.

4 Explain how we are able to visit those places. For example, to visit the top of Mount Everest, climbers need special warm clothing and extra oxygen to survive.

Remember

Copy and complete the sentences using these words:

**survive   different   food   humans
habitats**

All living things are adapted to the different **h**_____ where they live. Animals and plants would not **s**_____ if they were put in a **d**_____ habitat. Some animals can adjust to small changes in habitat if the **f**_____ supply is favourable. **H**_____ can adapt easily to most habitats.

A woodland

Figure 2 Some of the different habitats found in Britain.

A year in the life of a fox

Key words

life cycle   How an animal or plant lives, grows, develops and eventually dies

scavenging   Hunting and searching for food to eat

The urban fox

Figure 1 An urban fox looking for food.

Foxes usually live in the countryside. They eat a lot of different things including rabbits and small mammals. But many foxes now live in the cities. They are called urban foxes. Sometimes you can hear them at night. They make a sound like a young baby screaming. This is their mating call. They live by **scavenging** off the rubbish that humans put out and on any small mammals they can catch. The urban fox has learned to survive in the cities. People driving home late at night often see urban foxes on the roads.

Where do we find foxes?

The red fox is found in lots of different countries. It is a common sight in the countryside and is becoming more and more common in our towns and cities.

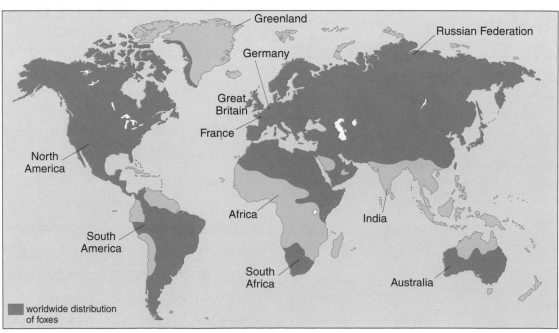

worldwide distribution of foxes

Figure 2 Where foxes are found around the world.

Question

1 In which countries are red foxes found?

Figure 3 A female fox (vixen) with her cubs.

The life cycle of a fox

How an animal or plant lives, grows, develops and eventually dies can be summed up in what we call a **life cycle**.

Month	What happens
January	Mating takes place
February March	↓ Cubs born
April May June	↓ Cubs often relocated to other dens
July	Cubs ready to leave their den
August	Grey fur replaced by red fur
September	Cubs fully grown
October	Male foxes fight amongst themselves
November December	↓

Table 1 The life cycle of a fox

Human life cycle

Humans have a life cycle. Our life cycle starts when fertilisation takes place. A baby is then born, it grows into a child, then a teenager, and finally an adult. Humans can live to a very old age.

Questions

2 Why do you think adult male foxes fight during October/November?

3 Why would the female fox (vixen) move the cubs to different dens?

4 Why might a young cub's coat colour be different from that of an adult?

Remember

Copy and complete the sentences using these words:

together   adapt   mate   food

Animals have to **a**_____ to changes in the weather and environment. All animals **m**___ and produce young when there is a good supply of food. Often they work **t**_____ to gather **f**____ and to rear their young.

Food chains and webs

Key words

consumer   Animals that eat other animals or plants

food chain   A list of plants and animals that shows how energy is transferred

food web   Lots of food chains linked together

photosynthesis   The way in which plants make their own food using water, carbon dioxide and the energy from sunlight to make sugar

producer   Green plants that make their own food by photosynthesis

Food chains

Very few animals eat only one type of food. Most animals, including humans, eat lots of different foods. Many **food chains** can be linked together forming **food webs**. Food chains and webs show us how energy is transferred from one living organism to another.

Making food chains and webs is quite a recent idea. In the 1920s Charles Elton, a biologist, was looking at how plants and animals lived and survived in the arctic, at a place called Bear Island. There were only a few plants and animals for him to study. He found that the biggest animal, the arctic fox, ate smaller birds. The birds ate insects and insects fed off leaves. The plants produced their own food by **photosynthesis**. He called his description a food chain. The arrows in a food chain show the direction that the energy is being passed, not what eats what.

Figure 1 The food chain on Bear Island. Plants → insects → sandpipers → arctic fox.

Questions

1   Where do plants get their energy from to produce their own food?

2   Put the following plants and animals into simple food chains
   a) human, grass, cow
   b) greenfly, cat, rose, bird

3   What do the arrows in a food chain show?

Step number	Name	Plant/animal type
1	**Producer** Something that makes or produces its own food.	Green plants.
2	**Primary** consumer Primary means first and consumer means to eat. This level contains animals that eat plants!	Insects and herbivores (animals that only eat plants).
3	**Secondary consumer** At this level the animals are usually larger (but not always). They will hunt other animals.	Usually carnivores (animals that eat other animals) and omnivores (animals that eat both plants and animals).

Table 1

Food webs

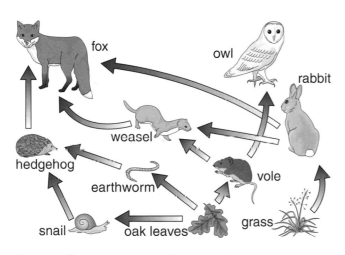

Figure 2 A woodland food web

Food webs give scientists a better idea of who eats whom in real life. Food webs can be very complicated. Like food chains they always start with plants that make their own food.

Questions

4 What do the following words mean? herbivore, carnivore, omnivore

5 Are most humans herbivores, carnivores or omnivores?

6 How many food chains can you make from the food web in Figure 2. Copy them into your exercise book.

Remember

Choose the correct word from each pair and copy and complete the paragraph in your exercise book

In the 1920s Charles Elton described who ate what and whom on Bear Island. He called this a **food/gold** chain. The first part of a food chain always begins with a plant. We call plants **consumers/producers** because they make their own food. The next link in the chain is a **primary/secondary** consumer and the final link in a chain is a **primary/secondary** consumer. When we link food chains together we make **food/spiders** webs.

Survival!

Meerkats

Many plants and animals have had to develop ways of protecting themselves from being eaten by others. Animals that hunt, kill and eat other animals are called **predators**. Animals that are hunted and eaten are called **prey**.

Look at the photos of the plants and animals. Then look at the descriptions a) to i) on the next page. Match the description of how it tries to protect itself, or how it tries to capture its food, with the name of the plant and animal. Make a table in your exercise book, like the one below and put the names of the animals in the first column and the correct description in the second column.

Name of animal	How is animal adapted to survive

A bat

An eagle

A spider

Chillies

Cacti

A dover sole

A stick insect

A snowshoe hare in summer (left) and winter (right)

a) These animals keep a look out for prey and their fur is similar in colour to the surrounding earth.

b) This animal is flat and similar in colour to its surroundings.

c) This animal changes its coat so that it can hide all year around.

d) This plant can burn the mouth when eaten raw. It also has a bright colour to warn others not to eat it.

e) This animal has a beak and talons to catch its prey.

f) This animal disguises itself like part of a plant to avoid being eaten.

g) This animal sets a trap to catch its prey.

h) This animal makes a high pitched sound and hears its prey when the sound bounces back.

i) This plant has spines that stop large animals from eating it.

Finishing off!

Remember

In this chapter we've looked at plants and animals in different parts of the world and how they survive. Where plants and animals are naturally found is called a **habitat**. A penguin's habitat is usually the cold Antarctic. They have a thick feathery coat that traps air to keep them warm. They also have a thick layer of fat to help them keep warm.

Copy and complete the following passage using the words supplied.

**predators   habitats   cactus
primary   carnivores   animals
urban fox   spines   eaten**

Different **h**_____ support different plants and **a**_____. In the desert, plants such as a **c**_____ will have thick fleshy stems that

hold a lot of water. The cactus has small, modified leaves that look like **s**_____. They stop water evaporating and protect the plant from being **e**_____. Some animals and plants can adapt to different habitats, such as the **u**_____ **f**____. It has learned to live in the city instead of its native countryside

Choose the correct word from each pair and copy the completed paragraph into your exercise book.

Plants are called **producers/consumers** because they make their own food. They do this by a process called **cooking/photosynthesis**. Animals that eat only plants are called herbivores. They are **primary/secondary** consumers. Animals that eat other animals are called secondary consumers or **carnivores/vegetarians**. Plants and animals are found in food chains. A food chain shows how the energy from the Sun is transferred from plants to animals and on to other animals.

Questions

1   Take a new page in your exercise book. Make a list of all the Key Words from the boxes in this chapter down the side. Take two lines per word. Try to write the meaning of each word without looking. Then go back and fill in any you did not know or got wrong.

Web sites to visit:

Food chains and webs
http://www.marietta.edu/~biol/102/ecosystem.html#Energyflowthrough theecosystem3

Animal Adaptations
http://scrtec.org/track/tracks/t06019.html

CHAPTER 11

Chemical change

Starter Activity
Water

Water is a strange substance.

- It expands when it freezes – no other liquid does that.

- It dissolves a big range of substances.

- It passes in and out of living cells easily (try sitting in the bath too long!).

But, it's the most common substance on the Earth.

Our bodies are 70% water. Our life is based on water. Our blood, our nerves, our digestion are all watery processes. Plants and animals cannot exist without water.

It's not a coincidence that water freezes at 0 °C and boils at 100 °C. It was the properties of water that were used to fix these points in our temperature scale.

Life is best suited to places where it finds land **and** water.

Questions

1 What is solid water called?

2 Name three substances that dissolve in water.

3 Explain simply why rain falls and where the water has come from to make rain.

4 Why does steam condense on cold windows?

5 Why do we sweat?

6 Why are tap water and rain water not totally pure water?

What munches metal?

11.1

Key words

hydrochloric acid Strong acid found in the stomach

hydrogen Gas given off when acids react with metal

sulphuric acid Strong acid found in car batteries

Questions

1 What happens when the magnesium is first put in the acid?

2 What happens to the solid magnesium metal in the end?

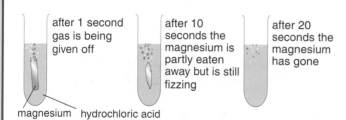

Figure 1 Alarm bells, warning sirens – you've seen it on TV. The saliva of the space monster is eating through the deck of the ship. Everyone's going to ...

The story in the picture is not totally true. Most metals react slowly with acids. The acid dissolves the metal and gets neutralised. In the reaction **hydrogen** gas is produced.

after 1 second gas is being given off

after 10 seconds the magnesium is partly eaten away but is still fizzing

after 20 seconds the magnesium has gone

magnesium hydrochloric acid

Figure 2 This is what happens when magnesium reacts with hydrochloric acid.

Testing for hydrogen

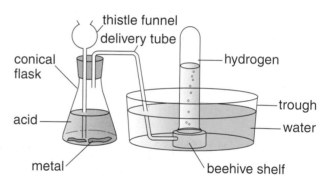

a) Hydrogen is a very light gas and it escapes easily.

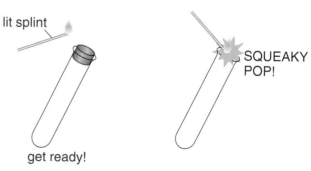

b) Keep the gas in the test tube with a bung.

c) Light with a splint. It will burn with a squeaky pop if it is hydrogen.

Figure 3

magnesium + hydrochloric acid → magnesium chloride + hydrogen
(the metal)   (the acid)   (the salt)   (the gas)

A Trekkies problem

Figure 4 Baghi is testing acids in the lab.

Baghi was sure Star Trek was right and all metals would dissolve in acid. He tried four metals and two acids. He chose **hydrochloric acid** and **sulphuric acid**. He knew these were strong acids.

Here are his results:

Camel urine is a liquid that is very corrosive to aeroplanes. If aeroplanes are carrying camels, their urine will eat through the metal floor!

Metal	Hydrochloric acid	Sulphuric acid
zinc	fizzed steadily	fizzed steadily
copper	nothing happened	nothing happened
magnesium	fizzed very quickly and dissolved	fizzed very quickly and dissolved
iron	fizzed slowly	fizzed slowly

Table 1 Baghi's results.

Remember

Copy and complete the sentences using these words:

**hydrogen   copper   acid
magnesium   squeaky pop**

M_____ metal dissolves in an **a___**.

It fizzes and the gas is **h_____**. The test for hydrogen is it burns with a **s_____ p___**.

But some metals such as **c_____** do not react with acids.

Questions

3 Do all metals get changed by acids?

4 How can Baghi do a test for hydrogen?

5 The magnesium disappeared in his test. Would the zinc and iron have done the same if they were left long enough?

Making a fizz

Testing for carbon dioxide

Carbon dioxide is the fizz gas that you see when marble reacts with any acid. The gas is colourless and it does not smell. How can you tell it is carbon dioxide?

Figure 1 When the marble is added to the hydrochloric acid, it fizzes as carbon dioxide gas is given off.

Marble is a beautiful stone. It is used to make statues. Marble is a chemical called calcium carbonate.

All **carbonates** will react with acids. The acid particles rip the carbonates up, but are chemically changed when they do it. The bits left over make a salt and **carbon dioxide** gas is given off.

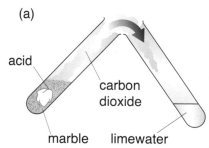

(a)

acid

carbon dioxide

marble   limewater

Carbon dioxide is heavier than air so it can be poured from one test tube to another

(b)

Shake the limewater and the gas together with a bung in the end of the test tube

limewater has gone milky, so we know the gas is carbon dioxide

Figure 2 You use limewater to test for carbon dioxide.

calcium carbonate + hydrochloric acid → calcium chloride + water + carbon dioxide
                                              (the SALT)   (the GAS)

Questions

1 What do you see when an acid reacts with marble?

2 What is the name of the gas given off?

3 What happens to the acid particles?

Put about 5 cm³ of **limewater** (calcium hydroxide solution) into a test tube. Carbon dioxide is a heavy gas. It can be poured into the test tube from the reacting mixture.

Put a cork in the test tube and shake it. Carbon dioxide gas will make the limewater go white and cloudy. No other gas does this.

Is there a pattern?

Figure 3 Luis is testing acids. He is wearing goggles to protect his eyes.

Luis knew there was a whole range of chemical substances, all of which had names ending in '-ate'. There were carbonates, sulphates, nitrates. He tested them with acid. He asked his teacher first. She told him it was safe so long as he wore goggles on his eyes.

Remember

Copy and complete the word grid. Use the clues to find the hidden word. Some letters are done for you.

Limewater goes _____

Carbonates react with _____

Using acid, you must be _____

The solid substances that fizz are

_____

Use _____ water in the test

Put the limewater in a ____ tube

Word grid

		m			k		
				c			
	c				f		
					a	t	e	s
			l				
	t						

Substance	What he saw when he added acid	Result of test with limewater
magnesium carbonate	fizz of gas and substance dissolved	limewater turned milky
magnesium sulphate	substance dissolved	no effect
iron carbonate (brown)	fizz of gas and substance dissolved	limewater turned milky
iron nitrate	substance dissolved	no effect
copper carbonate	fizz of gas and substance dissolved	limewater turned milky
copper nitrate	substance dissolved	no effect
sodium carbonate	fizz of gas and substance dissolved	limewater turned milky
sodium sulphate	substance dissolved	no effect

Table 1 What Luis found out.

Questions

4 How do you test a gas to see if it is carbon dioxide?

5 How many of the substances had carbonate names?

6 How many of the substances gave off carbon dioxide?

A nice change

Pancakes

Figure 1   In the café, Mandy is making pancakes.

1   Mandy mixes the egg, flour and milk until creamy smooth. She adds salt to taste.
2   She melts a little fat in a hot pan.
3   She pours in a little of the mixture and cooks it for about 30 seconds on each side.

Mandy can see changes take place as she makes the pancakes.

● When she heats the fat it loses its shape and turns into a liquid.

● When she cooks the pancake mix, it turns from a liquid to a solid and keeps its shape.

These are two different types of change.

When fat is heated it melts. When it cools again it **solidifies**. This can happen over and over again. The solid changes into a liquid when it is hot and changes back to a solid again when it cools. This is a **physical change**.

But when pancake mix is heated, the liquid turns into a solid shape. When it cools, it stays permanently in this shape. This is a **chemical change**.

Cooking changes

Lots of chemical changes happen in cooking.

Figure 2   Sugar is heated to make caramel toffee.

Figure 3   Bread is grilled to make toast.

Figure 4 Egg is cooked and goes solid.

The water cycle

In the water cycle there are lots of 'physical changes'. The water becomes solid (ice), liquid (water) and gas (water vapour) but it never stops being the same substance.

Questions

4   What makes the water evaporate from the sea?

5   Why does the water vapour become snow?

Questions

In your answers try to use scientific words like white or brown solid, thick or clear liquid.

1   a)   Describe what cooking fat looks like when it is solid.
    b)   What does it look like when it is liquid?

2   a)   Describe what pancake mix looks like before it is cooked.
    b)   What does it look like after it is cooked?

3   a)   Think of one other cooking change. Describe what the food looks like before and after cooking.
    b)   Has the food changed permanently?

Remember

Copy and complete the sentences using these words:

**melt   substance   chemical
physical   change**

When we heat substances they can **c**_____.

If they just **m**____ or boil, this is a **p**_____ change.

But sometimes the substance changes into a different **s**_____ .

This is a **c**_____ change.

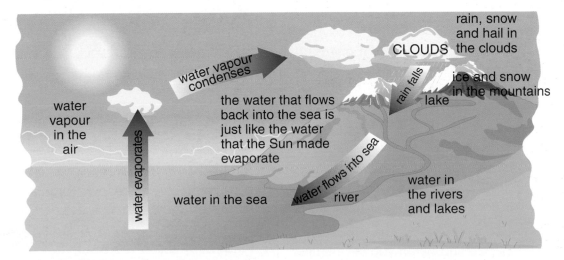

Figure 5 The water cycle.

Fire

Figure 1 When you strike a match, white fumes are made.

Fire has been our friend for over 400 000 years. Fire kept us warm. It frightened away wild animals. Some people worshipped it as a god.

Fire happens when a fuel reacts with **oxygen** gas in the air. The flames you can see are gases from the fuel mixing with the oxygen. When they do this, you get lots of energy. You can call this process burning or **combustion**.

Where does the heat come from?

Fuels are made of tiny particles. The new particles made in the chemical change contain less energy than the fuel particles. This is because some energy is released. Normally the energy is released as heat.

This is a **word equation** for the reaction in a Bunsen flame:

methane + oxygen →
                    carbon dioxide +water vapour

Propane

Figure 2 In this gas burner, propane is the fuel.

Propane is the proper name for the fuel we call bottled gas. It is made of tiny particles containing three carbon atoms and eight hydrogen atoms. Propane reacts with oxygen when it burns. You can draw a picture of what happens when a substance burns. You draw the particles as 'ball and stick' models.

Questions

1   What substance is needed for a fuel to be able to burn?

2   What is happening when you see flames?

The 'balls' are the atoms and the 'sticks' are the bonds which hold the atoms together. They don't really look like this, but it helps work out what is happening.

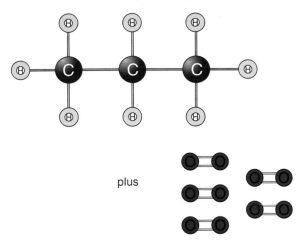

plus

Figure 3 Propane reacts with oxygen . . .

When the propane and oxygen have reacted (burnt), the atoms change partners and make new particles. They make carbon dioxide and water particles.

plus

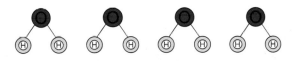

Figure 4 . . . to produce carbon dioxide and water.

Exactly the same atoms are there. They have just swapped round.

Remember

Copy and complete the sentences using these words:

**air   water   dioxide   fuels   flames
burning**

When **f____** burn they react with oxygen from the **a__**. The **f____** you see are the reaction happening.

Carbon **d_____** and **w____** vapour are made in burning. Combustion is the proper word for **b_____**.

Questions

3 Copy and fill in this table. Figures 3 and 4 will help you.

Type of atom	Number of atoms before reaction (Figure 3)	Number of atoms after reaction (Figure 4)
carbon		
hydrogen		
oxygen		

4 Write a word equation for the reaction of propane and oxygen.

Burning hot

Key words

fossil fuel   A fuel like coal or oil that was made underground, millions of years ago

fuel   Something that burns to release energy

Questions

1   Which fuels are used
    a)   at home on the barbecue?
    b)   in cars?
    c)   in big lorries?

2   Where did fossil fuels come from?

Fuels

Figure 1 Burning fuels to release energy.

Coal, gas and oil are **fossil fuels**. They are found in rocks underground. They were made over millions of years from the remains of dead animals and plants.

Burning **fuels** releases stored energy. This heats and lights up the place where the fire is.

This is the word equation for the chemical change when fossil fuels are burned.

Fighting fire

Figure 2 A pan on fire in the kitchen.

Figure 3 A house on fire.

fossil fuel + oxygen → carbon dioxide + water vapour + energy

Figure 4 A forest fire.

Home fires kill about 500 people a year in Britain. Most of these fires begin accidentally, but how does it happen?

A fire needs three things to get it going:

- fuel
- oxygen
- a high temperature.

These are often shown as the fire triangle

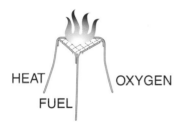

Figure 5 To get a fire going you need all the three things shown on the legs of the triangle.

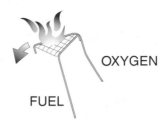

Figure 6 If you take away any one of the legs, the fire goes out. For example, to put out a chip pan fire, the fire fighter puts a wet blanket over it. This stops the supply of oxygen and the fire goes out.

Remember

Copy and learn this. Draw a picture to show what it means.

Oxygen is used up when fuels burn, and carbon dioxide and water vapour are made. This type of chemical reaction is called combustion.

To start a fire you need fuel, oxygen and a high temperature. One of these must be taken away to put out a fire.

Questions

3   Copy the table, and say which leg of the fire triangle collapses to put the fire out. One is done for you.

Method to stop fire	How does the fire triangle collapse?
a) Pour water on a charcoal barbecue	
b) Cut down the trees in the path of a forest fire	The fire stops because it runs out of fuel
c) Turn off the gas if there is an accident in the laboratory	
d) If a person's clothes are on fire, wrap them in a blanket or large coat	

Finishing off!

★ There are millions of different **materials** in the world. You use them all differently because they all have different **properties**.

★ Many materials change state when heated. They turn from **solid** to **liquid** (**melting**) or from liquid to **gas** (**boiling**). This is called a **physical change**.

★ The **water cycle** has physical changes. Water gets changed into vapour, then rain, then sometimes snow and ice, then back to water again.

★ Other materials change permanently when heated. These are **chemical changes**. Cooking is an example of chemical change.

★ We use **fuels** by burning them with **oxygen**. This transfers energy by heating and by light. This chemical change is called **combustion**. Many of our fuels are **fossil fuels** such as coal and oil.

★ When a fire gets out of control, you have to remove its fuel, its oxygen or its source of heating to make it go out.

1 Take a new page in your exercise book. Make a list of all the Key Words from the boxes in this chapter down the side. Take two lines per word. Try to write the meaning of each word without looking. Then go back and fill in any you did not know or got wrong.

2 What are the three states of matter?

3 What do you see when a material is melting?

4 How can you tell if a liquid is boiling?

5 What type of change happens to food when it is cooked?

6 Name three fossil fuels.

7 Explain why there are three ways to put out any fire.

Web sites to visit:

Center for the Study of Carbon Dioxide and Global Change
http://www.co2science.org

The Solar System

Starter Activity
Sunlight

We get our light from the Sun. When the Sun sets it goes dark. We then have to use electric lights or some other artificial light. The Earth rotates on its axis every 24 hours. So some parts are in the sunlight – daytime – and others are in shadow – night-time

The Sun is very big but it is a long way from Earth. If there was a motorway to the Sun it would take you more than 150 years to get there. The light from the Sun only takes about 8 minutes to reach us. Light travels at a very high speed!

The Sun is the source of nearly all our energy. We get our food from plants which absorb the energy from sunlight. They use a process called **photosynthesis**.

Questions

1 What happens to the height of the Sun in the sky from early morning to evening?

2 There is a lamppost in your street. It is a sunny day.
   a) At which time of day is the shadow shortest?
   b) At which time(s) of day is the shadow longest?

3 You see the Sun go down at 8.20 in the evening. At what time did the light you see leave the Sun?

4 Why do we have day and night?

Sunshine and shadows

Key words

lunar eclipse   The shadow of the Earth on the Moon

orbit   The circular path taken by an object round a planet or star

ray   The pathway of light

solar eclipse   The shadow of the Moon on the Earth

The Sun is the source of light that gives us daylight. Light travels out in all directions from the Sun.

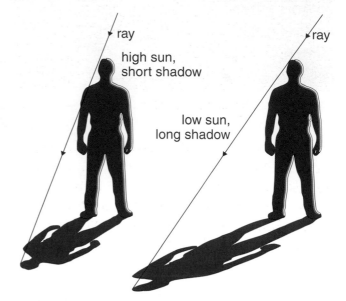

Figure 2 At midday the Sun casts a short shadow. In the evening the Sun is low down and casts a long shadow.

We can draw diagrams to show the straight pathways of light. The pathways are called **rays**.

Moon shadows

Figure 1 People make shadows in bright sunlight.

The people block the sunlight and make shadows on the ground. This is because light travels in straight lines and can't travel through them or round them.

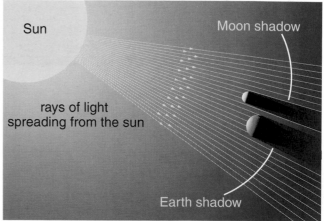

Figure 3 Shadows of the Earth and the Moon.

The Earth and the Moon make huge shadows. An astronaut going round the Earth goes in and out of its shadow.

The Sun can only shine on one half of the Moon. The other half is in darkness.

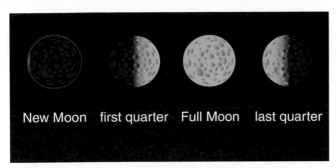

Figure 4 The phases of the Moon

New Moon   first quarter   Full Moon   last quarter

As the Moon **orbits** the Earth every 28 days, we see different amounts of the sunny and dark sides. Sometimes we see all of the sunny side of the Moon and then we call it a Full Moon. Sometimes we see just a thin slice of the sunny side and then we call it a New Moon.

Solar eclipse

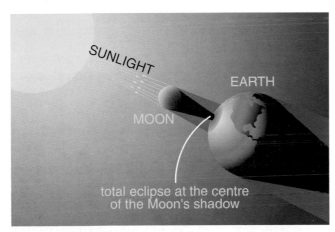

Figure 5 A solar eclipse.

Sometimes the shadow of the Moon falls on the Earth. It doesn't happen very often. It is called a **solar eclipse**.

Figure 6 The Moon passes in front of the Sun in the 1999 solar eclipse.

In 1999, the Sun, Moon and the Earth lined up. It went cold and dark for a few minutes in the middle of the day. The birds and animals went silent.

Lunar eclipse

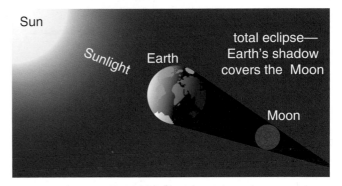

Figure 7 A lunar eclipse.

Sometimes the shadow of the Earth falls on the Moon. This is a **lunar eclipse**.

Questions

1 Why do we sometimes see a Full Moon and sometimes see a New Moon?

2 Explain what makes a solar eclipse happen.

Remember

Copy and complete the sentences. Use these words:

Earth   light   straight   rays   shadows   eclipse

The Sun is a source of l___. Light travels from the source and past the object in s___ lines. Some objects block the light and make s___. We can trace the pathways of the light with lines called r___. Sometimes the shadow of the Moon falls on the E___ and we get a solar e___.

Escape from the Earth

The force of gravity is a force that can act at a distance. It acts on all objects. Large objects like the Earth and the Sun exert large forces of gravity.

Stars and planets pull strongly on all other objects that are near to them, even if they are not touching. Gravity always pulls us down to the Earth's surface.

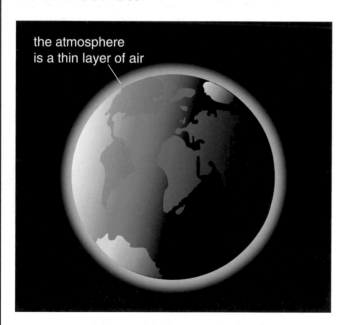

Figure 1 The atmosphere covers the Earth.

The Earth is a huge ball. It is surrounded by a thin layer of air which we breathe. This is called the Earth's **atmosphere**. It is gravity which stops this air from floating out into space.

Only a few animals and a few people have been outside the Earth's atmosphere.

Figure 2 Laika, the first dog in space.

The first animal to go into space was Laika, a Russian dog. In 1957 she was launched into space. The Russians wanted to see if an animal could survive the journey. There is no air in space so the spacecraft had to carry air to keep her alive.

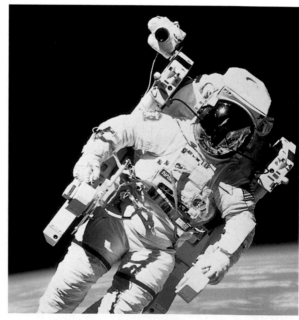

Figure 3 Above the atmosphere in empty space. Gravity still pulls on this astronaut. It keeps him in orbit round and round the Earth.

Astronauts escape from the Earth's atmosphere into space. But they don't escape from Earth's gravity. It holds them in orbit around the Earth.

Questions

1 What is the Earth's atmosphere?

2 Why did Laika's space capsule need to carry a supply of air?

Moon landing

Figure 4 Astronaut Buzz Aldrin sets foot on the Moon. The Moon's gravity holds him to the surface.

Neil Armstrong was the first man to set foot on the Moon in 1969. He took this photograph of Buzz Aldrin.

Figure 5 The Moon is smaller than the Earth so its gravity is much weaker.

The Moon has its own gravity. As the Moon is smaller than the Earth, its gravity is weaker. The Earth and Moon pull each other. The Moon orbits the Earth. They both orbit the Sun which is much bigger and has a stronger gravity.

Questions

3 Why is the gravity of the Moon weaker than the gravity of the Earth?

4 Describe what you think it would feel like to walk on the Moon like Neil Armstrong. You might include: how easy or difficult it is to walk, how you breathed, the view, the colour of the sky (*Hint*: see Figure 3) and your feelings on being so far from home.

5 Draw a picture of the Space Shuttle or a satellite. Show the rocket motors working.

Remember

Copy and complete the sentences. Use these words:

gravity   surface   bigger   atmosphere

All large objects exert a force of **g___**. The bigger the object, the **b___** the force.

The strong force of gravity holds us on the Earth's **s___**. Nobody has ever escaped from the influence of Earth's gravity. Some people have been above the **a___** where there is no air.

Planet hopping

The Sun is a huge star at the centre of a system of planets called the Solar System. The gravity of the Sun holds all the planets in orbit round it. The planet nearest the Sun is Mercury, then Venus, Earth and Mars. Next come the asteroids, thousands of rocks, some large some small. Then we have the gas giants, Jupiter and Saturn. Much further out are Uranus, Neptune and Pluto.

The planets do not give out light like the Sun. Instead we see them as bright specks in the night sky when light from the Sun is reflected off them. If you were to plot their movement against the stars they would seem to be wandering across the night sky. Some planets have their own moons in orbit round them.

Here is one way to help you remember the names of the planets in order. The first letter helps you think of the first letter of the planet's name

My **V**ery **E**xcellent **M**other **J**ust **S**ent **U**s **N**ine **P**izzas

Figure 1 This cartoon should help you remember the names of the planets.

A long time ago, in 1977, a spacecraft called Voyager 2 was launched. Its mission was to fly close to the planets. Here are some photographs that have been taken by spacecrafts like Voyager 2:

Figure 2 Mercury is nearest to the Sun. It is about the size of the Moon. The side facing the Sun is very hot – about 420 °C. It has no moons.

Figure 3 Venus is about as big as the Earth. It is hotter than Mercury – about 480 °C. At this temperature, lead would melt. It has a nasty atmosphere of sulphuric acid and carbon dioxide at high pressure. It has no moons.

Figure 4 Earth is a blue planet with clouds. It is just at the right distance from the Sun. Its temperature varies from −80 °C to +50 °C. It has water, oxygen and living things. It is the only planet with life. It has one moon.

Figure 5 Mars, the red planet, a cold desert of rocks. It has a very thin atmosphere of carbon dioxide. Its temperature ranges from $-120\,°C$ to $+20\,°C$. It has two moons.

Figure 6 Jupiter is the largest planet. Its gravity is very strong. It has no solid surface because it is mainly liquid hydrogen and helium at a temperature of 150 °C. The great red spot is a storm three times the size of the Earth. Jupiter has 16 moons.

Figure 7 Saturn is another gas giant. Its rings are made of billions of tiny bits of ice held in orbit by its gravity. It has more than 18 moons. Its temperature ranges from $-200\,°C$ to $-150\,°C$.

Figure 8 Uranus has a surface which is all liquid gas, mainly hydrogen, helium, ammonia and methane. Its temperature is $-210\,°C$. It has rings like Saturn and 15 moons.

Figure 9 Neptune, almost the twin of Uranus, is four times bigger than the Earth. It looks blue because of its thick atmosphere of cold methane gas. It has eight moons.

Figure 10 Pluto is very small. It is so far away that we do not know so much about it. The Sun's light is very weak. It is very cold, about $-230\,°C$. It has one moon. This photograph was taken by the Hubble Space Telescope.

Questions

1 Suppose you had to live on a planet other than Earth. Which would you choose? Say why you chose it.

2 Which planet (other than Earth) would you least like to live on. Give reasons for your choice.

Planets: how big? how far away?

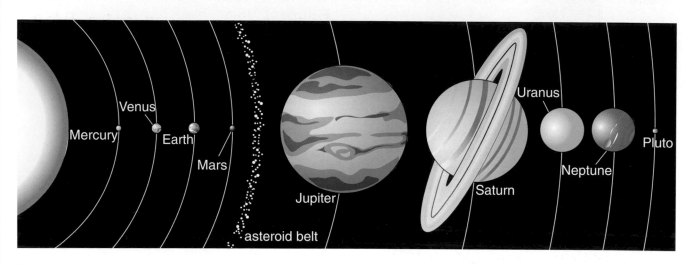

Figure 1 The picture shows how the sizes of the planets compare with the Earth. They don't lie in such a straight line as this.

The Solar System is made up of planets in orbit round the Sun. They are held in orbit by the Sun's gravity. Most of the planets have moons which are in orbit round them. They are held in orbit by each planet's gravity.

If there was no gravity, the Earth and other planets would escape from the Sun. We would lose the light and warmth of the Sun. Plants would not receive the energy they need to grow. They would die and we would starve and freeze in darkness.

Planet	Force of gravity
Mercury	4
Venus	9
Earth	10
Mars	4
Jupiter	26
Saturn	10
Uranus	8
Neptune	12
Pluto	1

Table 1 Force of gravity on a bag of sugar on the planet's surface, in newtons

Big planets have a stronger gravity than small ones.

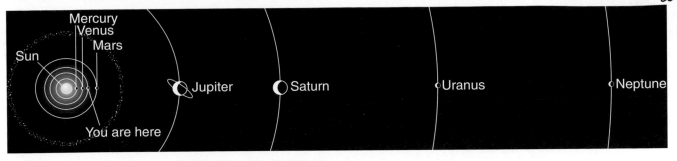

Figure 2 This picture shows how to compare the distances of the planets from the Sun. Pluto is too far away to fit on the page and the nearest star would be 1 km away!

Planet	Distance from Sun (km)
Mercury	58 000 000
Venus	108 000 000
Earth	150 000 000
Mars	228 000 000
Jupiter	778 000 000
Saturn	1430 000 000
Uranus	2870 000 000
Neptune	4500 000 000
Pluto	5900 000 000

Table 2 Average distances from the Sun

A model of the Solar System

If you made a scale model of the Solar System, you could use a grapefruit for the Sun. The Earth would be very small, about 1 mm in diameter. Mercury, Venus and Mars would be even smaller. Jupiter and Saturn would be about the size of a marble. Neptune and Uranus about 4 mm in diameter. Tiny Pluto, at 0.2 mm, would be smaller than a grain of salt.

Next you would need to go to a very large playing field with a long tape measure. The table shows the distances you would have to put your tiny planets from the grapefruit sized Sun.

Mercury = 4.8 m	Venus = 8.4 m	Earth = 12 m
Mars = 18 m	Jupiter = 60 m	Saturn = 114 m
Uranus = 228 m	Neptune = 360 m	Pluto = 468 m

If you wanted to include the nearest star, then you would have to put another grapefruit 3000 km (about 2000 miles) away!!

Questions

1 Which of the planets is most like the Earth in:
   a) its distance from the Sun
   b) the number of moons it has
   c) how heavy a bag of sugar (or anything else) is on its surface?

Remember

Copy and complete the sentences. Use these words:

**gravity planets strongest moons
Sun cold Venus Mercury Pluto**

The Solar System is made up of **p____** in orbit round the Sun. Most of the planets have **m____** in orbit round them. They are held in orbit by the force of **g____**. The biggest planets have the **s____** gravity.

The planets are at different distances from the **S____**. The closest one is **M____** and the furthest away is **P____**. Planets which are a long way from the energy of the Sun are **c____** and dark. The hottest planet is **V____**, the coldest is Pluto.

Seasons on the planets

Key words

hemisphere Half of a sphere. Usually refers to the halves of the Earth above and below the equator

Days and years on Earth

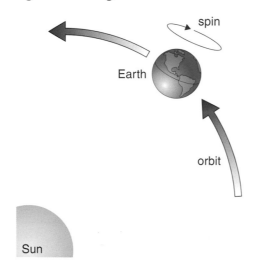

Figure 1 The Earth orbits and spins at the same time.

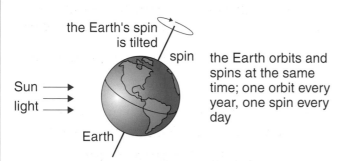

the Earth orbits and spins at the same time; one orbit every year, one spin every day

Figure 2 The Earth spins on its axis as it orbits the Sun. Its axis is on a tilt.

One complete spin of the Earth takes 24 hours and gives us day and night as we face towards and away from the Sun. One complete orbit is a year. In this time the Earth spins 365 and one quarter times. Every four years we have a leap year of 366 days.

The seasons on Earth

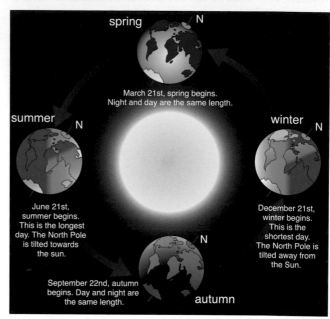

spring

March 21st, spring begins. Night and day are the same length.

summer

June 21st, summer begins. This is the longest day. The North Pole is tilted towards the sun.

winter

December 21st, winter begins. This is the shortest day. The North Pole is tilted away from the Sun.

September 22nd, autumn begins. Day and night are the same length.

autumn

Figure 3 It is the tilt of the Earth that gives us seasons.

The tilt in the Earth's spin means that for part of each year, the northern half is tilted towards the Sun. The northern half is called the northern **hemisphere**. At this time the Sun appears higher in the sky. It shines more overhead and the weather is warmer. It is summer. At the same time the southern half is tilted away from the Sun. The sunshine there is not as strong and it is winter.

Six months later when the Earth moves half way around the Sun, it's the southern hemisphere that gets the Sun more overhead. They have summer. Meanwhile the northern half is tilted away and there it is winter.

In winter the Sun does not rise so high in the sky. We do not spend so much of each day in the sunlight. It goes dark early in the afternoon and it gets light quite late in the morning.

Days and years on other planets

Different planets have different patterns of days, years and seasons.

The planets are all at different distances from the Sun. Mercury is the closest to the Sun and it takes the shortest time to go round it. Pluto is furthest from the Sun. Its orbit or year takes the longest.

once around the Sun

Planet	Length of planet's year	
Mercury	88 Earth days	= 1 Mercury year
Venus	225 Earth days	= 1 Venus year
Earth	365.25 Earth days	= 1 Earth year
Mars	687 Earth days	= 1 Mars year
Jupiter	12 Earth years	= 1 Jupiter year
Saturn	30 Earth years	= 1 Saturn year
Uranus	84 Earth years	= 1 Uranus year
Neptune	165 Earth years	= 1 Neptune year
Pluto	248 Earth years	= 1 Pluto year

Table 1 The length of each planet's year is the time it takes to travel once around the Sun.

one spin

Planet	Length of planet's day	
Mercury	1416 hours	= 1 Mercury day
Venus	5832 hours	= 1 Venus day
Earth	24 hours	= 1 Earth day
Mars	25 hours	= 1 Mars day
Jupiter	10 hours	= 1 Jupiter day
Saturn	10 hours	= 1 Saturn day
Uranus	11 hours	= 1 Uranus day
Neptune	16 hours	= 1 Neptune day
Pluto	6 hours	= 1 Pluto day

Table 2 A planet's day is the time it takes to spin round once on its axis.

Questions

1 Work out (to the nearest year) how old you would be if you lived on:
 a) Mercury (make 4 Mercury years = 1 Earth year)
 b) Mars
 c) Jupiter

2 How many times have you been round the Sun?

3 How many complete spins does the Earth make in one orbit round the Sun?

4 Why do we have seasons?

Remember

Copy and complete the sentences. Use these words:

**year tilted southern seasons
spin darkness away hemisphere**

The time that the Earth takes to go round the Sun is called one **y____**. The length of time that the Earth takes to make one **s____** is called one Earth day. The spin of the Earth is **t____**. The tilt stays the same all year. Sometimes the northern half of the Earth is tilted towards the Sun. Six months later the **s____** half of the Earth is tilted towards the Sun. That is why we have **s____**. In winter we spend longer in **d____** because then it is our **h____** which is tilted **a____** from the Sun.

Finishing off!

Remember

★ The Sun is our natural source of light. Light travels to us in straight lines at high speed.

★ The force of **gravity** holds us on the Earth. The force of gravity also keeps the Moon in **orbit** round the Earth.

★ The Earth and the Moon are in orbit together around the Sun. The Sun's strong force of gravity holds all the planets in orbit.

★ The spin of the Earth carries us in and out of the light of the Sun every day.

★ The **tilt** of the Earth gives us the **seasons**. In summer we are tilted towards the Sun. In winter we are tilted away from the Sun.

★ We see the planets in the night sky because they reflect light from the Sun back to us.

Questions

1 Take a new page in your exercise book. Make a list of all the Key Words from the boxes in this chapter down the side. Take two lines per word. Try to write the meaning of each word without looking. Then go back and fill in any you did not know or got wrong.

2 Write a story about an imaginary journey through the Solar System. On your journey you can visit some of the planets. You could choose just one planet if you prefer. Here are some things you can include in your story:

How far did you travel? What was your spaceship like? What does the surface of the planet look like? What does the Sun look like – is it larger or smaller than it appears from Earth? How long are the days? Does it mean that you have to sleep during the day? Have you landed during the planet's night? If so, how long will it be before it comes light? You walk outside and pick up some things, are they heavier than on Earth? How strong is the planet's gravity? Is it easy or hard to walk? Is it safe outside – what protection do you need from the conditions on the planet? Can you see any of the planet's moons? Do you think any of the planets might have life on them?

Web sites to visit:

NASA Homepage
    http://www.nasa.gov/

Amazing Space Web-based Activities
    http://amazing-space.stsci.edu/

Voyager Project Home Page
    http://vraptor.jpl.nasa.gov/

Nine Planets – a guide to the Solar System
    http://www.nineplanets.co.uk/

Index

Index